Prime Rib

More Titles by the Author:

Jacob's Journey

My Morning Cup

Understanding Goose

Fruity Tunes and the Adventures of Rotten Apple

There's a Turkey at Your Door

Exploring a Woman's Value & Purpose

JEANIE SHAW

Printed in the United States of America
ISBN: 978-1494292928
Morning Cup Press

Cover design: Jennifer Maugel
Interior design: Thais Gloor

www.jeaniesjourneys.com

To my sisters:

Carolyn, whose creativity inspired me;
Kay, whose peace calmed me;
Barbara, whose big heart made me feel loved.

And to the loving memory of my friend,
Rebecca Christensen

Acknowledgments:

Thank you to Lory Demshar and Melanie Singh, who added helpful suggestions as we "team taught" many of these topics; the women in the Northern Worship Center who were so encouraging as they eagerly participated in the "Prime Rib" class; Elizabeth Thompson, my editor, who "gets me" and uses her God-given talents to make my words sound better; and my husband, who not only puts up with my crazy middle of the night typing...but also cheers me on.

Contents:

Introduction

There is something innately satisfying about finishing. Perhaps you let out a sigh of relief, or a feeling of accomplishment wells up inside. It feels good and right when something is finished. As a minister to women, I see countless needs in the lives of people around me, and it is often hard, at the end of the day, to feel like any of my work (really, God's work) is "finished." Perhaps that is why I like to write books. They have a last page—the end.

Even though God had made the broad and glorious universe—from the vast galaxies to the infinitesimal nanoparticles—he desired to create someone like himself. This would be someone he could walk with and talk with, and lavish his love upon. And so he created man. However, creation was not yet complete:

> The LORD God said, "It is not good for the man to be alone. I will make a helper suitable for him."
>
> Now the Lord God had formed out of the ground all the beasts of the field and all the birds of the air. He brought them to the man

to see what he would name them; and whatever the man called each living creature, that was its name. So the man gave names to all the livestock, the birds of the air and all the beasts of the field.

But for Adam no suitable helper was found. So the Lord God caused the man to fall into a deep sleep; and while he was sleeping, he took one of the man's ribs and closed up the place with flesh. Genesis 2:18–21

God knew all along that he would create woman. He had made the animals male and female. Perhaps, in his timing, he wanted to make sure that Adam knew how much he needed Eve. So God let him go it alone for a while—perhaps Adam lived in a messy "bachelor cave," surviving on under-seasoned food, feeling lonely with no one to roll her eyes at his jokes or hold him close at night—and then, when Adam had come to understand that something—some*one*—was missing, God put him to sleep while he skillfully and perfectly formed woman.

Woman was not an afterthought, made only because God found an extra rib lying around. God took a rib from man. We were fashioned in an extraordinary way.

"Then the LORD God made a woman from the rib he had taken out of the man, and he brought her to the man" (Genesis 2:22). Then creation was complete. And it was very good.

The word 'prime' can mean *of foremost importance, having great significance,* and *deserving the fullest consideration.*[1]

And so a *prime* rib would be a rib of first importance, of great significance, and worthy of the fullest consideration—hence the title for this book.

My desire is that through these pages you will come to understand in a deeper way how you were fashioned and designed by God with love and purpose.

Having ministered to women for the past forty years, these ten chapters include crucial convictions I have gained over the years—convictions that I believe are of utmost importance for women to know and live by. My prayer is that these pages will leave you with a greater understanding of your value and the role for which God created you. We were created with love, and with a God-given role and purpose. All of us can find fulfillment when we live the way God designed for us, and when we understand the height and depth and breadth of his love for us. When we live loved, we can live loving, and love living.

May we all come to grasp, as Paul prayed in Ephesians 3:17–19, "how wide and high and long and deep is the love of Christ, and to know this love that surpasses knowledge—that you may be filled to the measure of all the fullness of God."

Jeanie Shaw
January, 2014

Chapter 1

Designed With Love and Purpose

Do you ever struggle with believing that you are loved, and loveable? Do you look in the mirror and see only your imperfections? Do you recount the ways you should be a better parent, a better wife, a better friend, a better everything? Do you often compare yourself to others who seem to have it more together? Do you let your past and weaknesses define your worth, or let others' views of you define your value? If you do, it is crucial that you take the time to understand the way God sees you. When you understand and believe what he says about you, it changes everything.

God sees each of us as precious, created just as we were intended to be. He planned for us to be different from each other in many ways—as varied as the unique parts of our body—so that we would understand our need for each other (1 Corinthians 12:12–27).

Despite God's design and plan for our lives, many women struggle with believing that we are objects of God's affection. What is your view of God's love, and how did you get this view? Some of us have had absent fathers, or distant mothers, or parents who were *too* present—dictatorial, authoritarian, and controlling. Others of us have suffered physical, emotional, or verbal abuse. Many have suffered illness or loss. The list of painful experiences is endless, and the repercussions can be endless, too. They can affect our confidence, our happiness, and our spirituality. They can obscure our view of God. We may come to view him as a supernatural being who is distant and uninvolved. We may feel that we are unimportant or insignificant to him. We may think that God is actively involved in and concerned for other people's lives, but not ours. We may suspect that God is out to get us—to ruin what little happiness we have. We may decide that we do not believe in God at all . . . or even if we do still believe, we no longer trust him.

But I hope that as you read this book, you will allow the word of God to transform your view of him. Let go of the painful misconceptions life has taught you, and let the Bible teach you. Hear God's promises and declarations with open ears, an open mind, and an open heart.

God's Love Letter

In order to see ourselves through God's eyes, we must come to believe what he says about us. Consider the prophet Zephaniah's words in Zephaniah 3:17:

> The LORD your God is with you,
> > he is mighty to save.
> He will take great delight in you,
> > he will quiet you with his love,
> > he will rejoice over you with singing.

What an amazing thought—God takes delight in us and rejoices over us with singing. He does this for you and me.

> I waited patiently for the LORD;
> > he turned to me and heard my cry.
> He lifted me out of the slimy pit,
> > out of the mud and mire;
> he set my feet on a rock
> > and gave me a firm place to stand.
> He put a new song in my mouth,
> > a hymn of praise to our God.
> Many will see and fear
> > and put their trust in the LORD.
> Psalm 40:1–3

> By day the LORD directs his love,
> > at night his song is with me—
> > a prayer to the God of my life. Psalm 42:8

In Psalm 136, the words "His love endures forever" are repeated 27 times. God wants us to understand that he loves us!

The Bible, even with all the Old Testament's journeys and battles and the New Testament's accounts of the formation and growth of God's church, is really a love letter to us. Once we understand this fact, our motivation for learning the Bible changes. Our desire to know God changes. We go from a place where we view Bible study and prayer as a duty or simply a "church thing," to a place where we are thrilled by the privilege of walking and talking with God, who continually tells us of his love for us. I am reminded of the words of an old favorite hymn, "In the Garden" by C. Austin Miles:

I come to the garden alone
While the dew is still on the roses
And the voice I hear falling on my ear
The Son of God discloses.

He speaks, and the sound of His voice
Is so sweet the birds hush their singing,
And the melody that He gave to me
Within my heart is ringing.

I'd stay in the garden with Him
Though the night around me be falling,
But He bids me go; through the voice of woe
His voice to me is calling.

Chorus:
And He walks with me, and He talks with me,
And He tells me I am His own;
And the joy we share as we tarry there,
None other has ever known.[2]

Of utmost importance as we grow to understand God's plan and design for us as women, is the conviction that we are dearly loved by God. We are not accidents. As Genesis 2:22 tells us, we were hand-designed by God, made for relationship with him and others.

God longs for us to walk and talk with him, as he did with Eve many years ago. It may not always be in a quiet garden, as the song states. It may be when we are caught in traffic or when our kids are tired, hungry, and unhappy. God wants to comfort us when we are dealing with sick parents, sick children, or perhaps our own illness. When we are afraid, God longs for us to feel his strength. When we are sad, he desires to wipe the tears from our eyes. He desires to replace our loneliness with the presence of his company.

Take the time to be still with him and listen to his promises. Bask in his love for you. Hear him sing to you.

The longer that God's Spirit lives within us, the more we will continue to be fed by his word and strengthened by his family. We can then experience the inner peace he offers no matter what circumstances we face. We have something extraordinary to pass on to those whom our lives touch.

Unfortunately, as we will explore more specifically in the next chapter, Satan always desires to steal this relationship and feed us lies. Eve succumbed to the temptation, and as a result she felt ashamed and vulnerable. In her nakedness, she hid from God. Her relationship with God was affected. Some things never change. When we let Satan steal the relationship God intended for us to have with him, we, too, are left feeling vulnerable and distant.

God Comes Looking

But God came looking—and he's looking for us even now. God sought out Adam and Eve. He missed their fellowship, and he called out for them. Do you think he didn't know where they were? He can see everything, but he wanted them to know he was looking for them. They hid, as we all do when we have strayed from God—and yet God called out for them. God still comes looking for us, desiring a relationship with us:

> " 'For this is what the Sovereign LORD says: I myself will search for my sheep and look after them. As a shepherd looks after his scattered flock when he is with them, so will I look after my sheep. I will rescue them from all the places where they were scattered on a day of clouds and darkness.' " Ezekiel 34:11–12

> "From one man he made every nation of men, that they should inhabit the whole earth; and he determined the times set for them and the exact places where they should live. God did this so that men would seek him and perhaps reach out for him and find him, though he is not far from each one of us." Acts 17:26–27

God walked through the garden, calling out, "Where are you?" Eve finally answered and stood naked before him. Did God berate her, scream at her, or just give her the silent treatment? He could have—the whole heartbreaking scene was Eve's fault, after all. Instead he simply said, "How could you do such a thing?"

I try to imagine how God said this—and I'm guessing it was said with sadness and hurt, more than with anger. God wanted to know why she had rejected his love when he had shown her blessing upon blessing, and given her no reason to doubt him. This relationship was meant to be reciprocal. God did not wish to destroy Eve because of her fall. He came looking, wanting the relationship restored—back to the way he'd created it to be.

When we stray, when we hide, when we listen to lies, when we take control, when we are discontent, when we are insecure, when we feel worthless and think we have messed up too much, it is difficult to hear the voice of God. Can you still hear God calling for you? Can you imagine him saying to you, "How could you do such a thing? How can you not trust my love for you?" Can you hear the hurt in his voice?

Ezekiel 16:4–14 dramatically depicts God's tender love for us through an allegory; God describes his feelings toward his beloved Israel after she had wandered from his love:

> " 'On the day you were born your cord was not cut, nor were you washed with water to make you clean, nor were you rubbed with salt or wrapped in cloths. No one looked on you with pity or had compassion enough to do any of these things for you. Rather, you were thrown out into the open field, for on the day you were born you were despised.

" 'Then I passed by and saw you kicking about in your blood, and as you lay there in your blood I said to you, "Live!" I made you grow like a plant of the field. You grew up and developed and became the most beautiful of jewels. Your breasts were formed and your hair grew, you who were naked and bare.

" 'Later I passed by, and when I looked at you and saw that you were old enough for love, I spread the corner of my garment over you and covered your nakedness. I gave you my solemn oath and entered into a covenant with you, declares the Sovereign LORD, and you became mine.

" 'I bathed you with water and washed the blood from you and put ointments on you. I clothed you with an embroidered dress and put leather sandals on you. I dressed you in fine linen and covered you with costly garments. I adorned you with jewelry: I put bracelets on your arms and a necklace around your neck, and I put a ring on your nose, earrings on your ears and a beautiful crown on your head. So you were adorned with gold and silver; your clothes were of fine linen and costly fabric and embroidered cloth. Your food was fine flour, honey and olive oil. You became very beautiful and rose to be a queen. And your fame spread among the nations on account of your beauty, because the splendor I had given you made your beauty perfect, declares the Sovereign LORD.' "

Just like the woman in this story, Eve also forgot that God and his love were enough, and she went astray. She was left naked and ashamed. God understood that she had made herself vulnerable. The very thing God did for Eve, he did for Israel, and now also for us: He covers our shame.

When Eve stood before God in her vulnerability, he himself clothed her so that she would no longer feel ashamed. (Talk about "designer clothes!") God showed her the same tender mercy he would show toward Israel, the mercy he now offers us. He has designed clothes for us to cover our shame. As he did with Eve, he sacrificed something else from his creation to provide for us. He sacrificed an animal to clothe Eve, and his son to clothe us.

As Galatians 3:27 says, "For all of you who were baptized into Christ have clothed yourselves with Christ."

What do our God-given clothes look like? Colossians 3:12–16 describes the clothes made available to us through Jesus. Through him, we can clothe ourselves with compassion, kindness, humility, gentleness, patience, forgiveness, love, peace, thankfulness and relationships.

No matter how you have viewed God and viewed yourself up to this point, I pray that you will come to understand the immense love with which God designed you—this perspective changes everything. For when we live loved . . . we live loving, and we love living.

Taking it Deeper:

Designed In Love

1. What is your view of God? What experiences, people, and events in your life have shaped your view of God?

2. How do you view yourself? What factors in your life have shaped how you view yourself?

3. What difference might it make in your life if you were convinced that God loves you wholeheartedly and individually?

4. Read Ezekiel 16:4–14, Galatians 3:27, and Colossians 3:12. What spiritual clothing has God designed for you?

Chapter 2

Missing Out on God's Love

Eve had a good thing going. She had been lovingly designed by God, and he wanted to be close to her. He had given her the perfect mate, and a glorious place to live, with everything she and Adam could ever need for happiness and fulfillment. However, too soon along the way she believed a lie, and so she strayed from the plan God had for her life: she damaged her marriage, lost her home, and hurt her relationship with her Creator. We often refer to her actions as the "fall of man."

"Sin" is actually an archery term for "missing the mark." When we sin, we miss the mark God has set out for us—and we also miss out on his good plans for us. When sin entered the picture in Eden, Eve missed the mark of God's perfect plan for her. How did this happen? Eve's temptations are not so very different from our own.

Eve was living a safe, comfortable, happy life in Eden—close to God and her husband, with all of her needs fully met. But then Satan came for a visit. His intention was clear from the beginning: to hurt what was most valuable to God—the people God had created, God's offspring. Satan approached Eve the same way he approaches us: masquerading as an angel of light, slick and full of deception. As a fallen angel, he hates and opposes God and will do everything in his means to hurt and destroy God's beloved.

Satan's Lies

Satan lied to Eve by making her doubt the truth of what God had said to her. He used the same technique, without success, with Jesus (Matthew 4:1–11). Satan continues to lie to us today (2 Corinthians 11:14–15), and just as he did with Jesus, he tempts us with the lust of the eyes, the lust of the flesh, and the pride of life:

> Do not love the world or anything in the world. If anyone loves the world, the love of the Father is not in him. For everything in the world—the cravings of sinful man, the lust of his eyes and the boasting of what he has and does—comes not from the Father but from the world. The world and its desires pass away, but the man who does the will of God lives forever. 1 John 2:15–17

As the prince of this world (John 12:31; 14:30), Satan uses the things of this world and our fleshly nature to tempt us to be unfaithful to God. Satan tempts us in several basic ways: He makes what this world offers look good and feel good, and then he tells us we deserve more than we have.

Through cunning deception Satan convinced Eve that God was holding back something valuable from her. She soon felt that what God had already given her was not enough. Although Eve had been given a perfect place to live, a purpose, and a marriage made in heaven, she assumed she knew what was best for her own life—and after all, she deserved more. Satan twisted the very words of God, and Eve failed to hold to the truth that God had given her. Whenever we feel we deserve more, whenever we become ungrateful and discontent, whenever we forget what God has said in his word, we become prime targets for Satan's lies.

What are some of Satan's most common lies to us as women?

> *You aren't valuable; you aren't really loved. You don't measure up.*
>
> *You don't have what you need—you need a man, more money, more talent, more beauty, more sex appeal.*
>
> *You know what you need more than anyone else knows.*

Satan tempts us in the same ways he tempted Eve. He makes his ways look good, feel good, and appeal to our pride. We will always face temptation, but we don't have to follow through with sin.

As a modern-day proverb puts it, "We can't help it when birds fly around our head . . . but we can keep them from building a nest in our hair." Temptation itself is not sin; it is a reminder that we are in the battle. The Bible puts it this way:

> Blessed is the man who perseveres under trial, because when he has stood the test, he will receive the crown of life that God has promised to those who love him.
>
> When tempted, no one should say, "God is tempting me." For God cannot be tempted by evil, nor does he tempt anyone; but each one is tempted when, by his own evil desire, he is dragged away and enticed. Then, after desire has conceived, it gives birth to sin; and sin, when it is full-grown, gives birth to death.
>
> Don't be deceived, my dear brothers. Every good and perfect gift is from above, coming down from the Father of the heavenly lights, who does not change like shifting shadows. He chose to give us birth through the word of truth, that we might be a kind of first fruits of all he created. James 1:12–19

The Truth About Lies

Since Satan continues to tempt us, it is crucial for us to become wise to the methods he uses to trick us. Lies come in many shapes and sizes. The best way to spot a lie is to know what is true. For example, counterfeit money has been around for a long time because so many people are fooled by its appearance—it looks so similar to real money. If I were to look at different pieces of counterfeit money all day, I would likely become increasingly confused as to what was real and what was fake. Likewise, the more we observe popular philosophy, pop culture, advertising, and even various brands of theology, the more we become confused as to what is true and what is not. Our culture tells us that whatever feels comfortable and looks right to us is true for us. This is one of Satan's biggest lies.

We must learn to define truth the way God defines truth. But how do we know what is true? Consider these ways to spot the "real thing" in money and in God's word:

In order to spot counterfeit money you must know what true money looks like. Here are three tips for recognizing "true" money:

- Hold currency up to bright lighting. If it's a good bill, you'll see a hologram on the face-up side of the bill. Ideally, both of the images should match up perfectly. Looking through the light should reveal a thin vertical strip.

- Take any $10, $20 or $50 note and move it back and forth (tilting it as you do). You should notice a number in the lower right-hand corner. If the bill is genuine, you should be able to see a shift in the colors.

- Hold a bill up to ultraviolet light. Each denomination glows in its own color.

In order to spot Satan's lies, we must become familiar with God's truth as delivered in his word. Here are three tips for learning the truth—which is of far greater significance than learning how to spot legitimate money:

- Read the Bible regularly. Don't assume you already know it.

- Read it in context: Who is writing? Who is this written to? What was the situation at the time of writing?

- Apply the Scriptures to your life: What is this saying to me? Where do I fall short, and how can I adapt my life to God's plan, rather than adapting God to my way of living?

Satan will always try to distort the truth and make it look real. He is a deceiver and the father of lies.

> Jesus said to them, "If God were your Father, you would love me, for I came from God and now am here. I have not come on my own; but he sent me. Why is my language not clear to you? Because you are unable to hear what I say. You belong to your father, the devil, and you want to carry out your father's desire. He was a murderer from the beginning, not holding to the truth, for there is no truth in him. When he lies, he speaks his native language, for he is a liar and the father of lies. Yet because I tell the truth, you do not believe me! John 8:42–45

> The great dragon was hurled down—that ancient serpent called the devil, or Satan, who leads the whole world astray. He was hurled to the earth, and his angels with him. Revelation 12:9

When we believe the lies Satan tells us, our thinking becomes distorted in many ways. As a result, we become envious, insecure, and reap all sorts of relational difficulties. We are then unable to access and accept God's grace as it really is.

> At one time we too were foolish, disobedient, deceived and enslaved by all kinds of passions and pleasures. We lived in malice and envy, being hated and hating one another. But when the kindness and love of God our Savior appeared, he saved us, not because of righteous things we had done, but because of his mercy. He saved us through the washing of rebirth and renewal by the Holy Spirit, Titus 3:3–5

What are some truths that we, as women, need to remember?

- We were purposely and lovingly created in God's image. He loves us deeply, so much so that he willingly gave his only son to die in our place. Mothers, let that one sink in. This is unthinkable love—beyond my imagination.

- Our hearts are deceitful. We are sinners. We have messed up over and over again. Romans

3:23 states this clearly, as do many other Bible verses. And even though we are dearly loved and created in God's image, we still fall for Satan's lies. Jeremiah 17:9 states a truth we can often miss:

"The heart is hopelessly dark and deceitful, a puzzle that no one can figure out. But I, God, search the heart and examine the mind. I get to the heart of the human. I get to the root of things. I treat them as they really are, not as they pretend to be." Jeremiah 17:9-10 (MSG)

• When we learn and follow the truth, the truth will set us free.

Whoever said that God would want you to "trust your heart" or "follow your heart" simply does not know the Bible. We get into all sorts of trouble when we let our hearts lead us away from the truth of the Bible. We can too easily follow our hearts into disobedience of God.

We become our own worst enemies when we don't willingly acknowledge that we are sinners in need of God's grace. How easy is it for you to acknowledge your weaknesses and sins? For women who have the courage to share their sins and struggles, not only do they more fully understand and experience God's grace, but they are also better able relate and connect with others.

I realize that I have strong "perfectionist" tendencies. I like to know how to do things and I like to do them well, or . . . uh . . . maybe perfectly. Unfortunately, until I was about forty years old, I found it difficult to enumerate and share my sins and weaknesses with others, because I didn't want to mess up—thinking that God expected perfection. I focused on "just doing the right thing," which is actually a good and right practice—unless it causes us to be self-righteous and judgmental. I tended toward the latter. As a result, I was shut down, defensive, and deceived. Through much prayer and Bible reading—along with the input from other people who I allowed into my life (even though I was sometimes kicking and screaming in my heart)—I came to understand my weakness and became determined to learn this new "language of vulnerability." A friend helped me understand that it's "okay to mess up." That's what grace is all about. Of course, grace is not a license to sin, but if I don't feel the need for God's grace, I am merely a Pharisee.

I had to practice vulnerability. I would ask those around me, "How am I doing at being vulnerable?" I asked this again and again. For me, it was like learning a new language. Now, twenty years later, I am often told that vulnerability has become my strength! I have developed deep and close friendships—something not possible until you let others know the "real you."

Sometimes, women will readily admit their weaknesses, but still won't allow others into their lives to help them change those weaknesses. How do you respond, in your heart of hearts, when someone shares an observation about your life that they believe needs growth?

If we are like Eve (and we are), we will tempted to respond like her—we blame and hide. We may be quick to deflect the blame onto someone else, finding a reason why our sins and weaknesses are someone else's fault. Perhaps we don't like the way someone has spoken to us, or we don't trust that they have our best interest in mind. We wrongly assume that *they* are the problem. We may blame the "messenger," thinking they just don't understand us or don't trust us. Or, we may attack the messenger with our anger, hoping we can intimidate them until they leave us alone.

We may try to hide by disengaging from others who see our weaknesses, or by avoiding situations where heart-to-heart conversations may take place. We can also hide by choosing to only share our victories and "positive status updates." We avoid sharing sins from our past or present, thinking that other people would think less of us if they knew what was really inside of us. While we don't need to dwell on our past or present sins, hiding them makes them difficult to overcome, and alienates us from the people who can likely help us the most. When we hide or blame, we tell others that we don't want or need their help in our life. We can also "hide" by learning the art of manipulating the focus away from ourselves, thus avoiding conversations that could expose our weaknesses.

When a woman is insecure and unwilling to hear helpful input for her life, she leaves herself in a very vulnerable position. This combination of insecurity and pride builds thick, defensive walls, making it difficult for others—including God—to penetrate. Be brave enough to listen to others who muster the courage to come to you with concerns about your life. (And don't assume this warning does not apply to you—as we are easily deceived!) Continually seek input for your life—using words like "help me understand what you are saying," or "what do you see in my interactions with others (including my husband and children) that I could improve?" or "what are areas where you think I need to grow?" We never outgrow this need for input in our lives. I became a Christian as a young teen, and I turn sixty years old next month, and I still ask these questions regularly. I don't ever want to "outgrow" this practice. Why wouldn't I want to be a better daughter to God, a more loving wife, a wiser and more loving mother, and a better friend? Why wouldn't you?

The truth is that the truth is our friend—it is not our enemy. Lies are our enemy. The truth sets us free . . . always (John 8:32).

Who Do We Listen To?

Eve listened to the wrong voice. She was enticed by false words and promises. We can learn from her mistakes. The Bible gives us a number of strategies for dealing with Satan and his schemes:

> Submit yourselves, then, to God. Resist the devil, and he will flee from you. James 4:7

> Be self-controlled and alert. Your enemy the devil prowls around like a roaring lion looking for someone to devour. Resist him, standing firm in the faith, because you know that your brothers throughout the world are undergoing the same kind of sufferings. And the God of all grace, who called you to his eternal glory in Christ, after you have suffered a little while, will himself restore you and make you strong, firm and steadfast. To him be the power for ever and ever. Amen. 1 Peter 5:8–11

Temptation may feel strong, but God is stronger—and he promises to help us resist the devil when he comes knocking.

I love this famous Native American story, because it paints a vivid picture of biblical principles at work:

> An old Cherokee told his grandson, "My son, there is a battle between two wolves inside us all. One is Evil. It is anger, jealousy, greed, resentment, inferiority, lies, and ego. The other is Good. It is joy, peace, love, hope, humility, kindness, empathy, and truth."
>
> The boy thought about it and asked, "Grandfather, which wolf wins?"

The old man quietly replied, "The one you feed."

When Eve listened to Satan, and fed his lies inside her own heart, she lost the perfect relationship with God for which she had been created. As a result, she felt vulnerable—filled with shame and insecurity—and she hid from the presence of God.

God rebuked the devil for his schemes, and described for Eve the consequences of her sin. Sin always has penalties. Even though God was hurt by Eve's sin, and she paid the price for her mistakes, God never quit loving her. We are all left with consequences of sin in our relationship with God, but he never stops loving us, and he can always make us new. God sought Eve, and when he found her, he clothed her and forgave her. She was still the object of his love and affection. We see this same heart of persistence throughout the Scriptures.

> Praise the LORD, O my soul;
>   all my inmost being, praise his holy name.
> Praise the LORD, O my soul,
>   and forget not all his benefits—
> who forgives all your sins
>   and heals all your diseases,
> who redeems your life from the pit
>   and crowns you with love and compassion,
> who satisfies your desires with good things
>   so that your youth is renewed like the
>   eagle's.
>
> The LORD works righteousness
>   and justice for all the oppressed.

He made known his ways to Moses,
  his deeds to the people of Israel:
The LORD is compassionate and gracious,
  slow to anger, abounding in love.
He will not always accuse,
  nor will he harbor his anger forever;
he does not treat us as our sins deserve
  or repay us according to our iniquities.
For as high as the heavens are above the
    earth,
  so great is his love for those who fear him;
as far as the east is from the west,
  so far has he removed our transgressions
    from us.
As a father has compassion on his children,
  so the LORD has compassion on those
    who fear him;
for he knows how we are formed,
  he remembers that we are dust.
Psalm 103:1–14

Or do you not know that the wicked will not inherit the kingdom of God? Do not be deceived: Neither the sexually immoral nor idolaters nor adulterers nor male prostitutes nor homosexual offenders nor thieves nor the greedy nor drunkards nor slanderers nor swindlers will inherit the kingdom of God. And that is what some of you were. But you were washed, you were sanctified, you were justified in the name of the Lord Jesus Christ and by the Spirit of our God. 1 Corinthians 6:9–11

> Praise be to the God and Father of our Lord
> Jesus Christ! In his great mercy he has given
> us new birth into a living hope through the
> resurrection of Jesus Christ from the dead,
> and into an inheritance that can never perish,
> spoil or fade—kept in heaven for you, who
> through faith are shielded by God's power
> until the coming of the salvation that is ready
> to be revealed in the last time. 1 Peter 1:3–5

In order to live in a way that reflects God's love for us we must:

- Remember we were created as objects of God's affection.

- Understand where our view of ourselves comes from.

- Know what Satan is trying to do when he tells us lies.

- Recognize Satan's lies, and know and believe the truths of God. Remember that Satan masquerades as an angel of light.

- Know where discontent and ingratitude lead, and how they show themselves in our lives.

- Understand the progression of lies that most often tempt us (James 1:12–19).

- Decide which wolf we'll feed (Romans 12:21).

- Remember that God can make us new.

Don't miss out on God's plan for your life. His word is a love letter to you. He longs to hold you close to his heart and lavish his love on you. He longs for your fellowship, and for your whole heart. Only in this love will you fill the longing in your soul.

Taking It Deeper:

Missing Out on God's Love

1. How has your past shaped the way you view yourself?

2. What are some of the primary lies Satan tells you?

3. What are three ways you can "feed the good wolf"?

Chapter 3

Am I Really "the Help"?

Does the thought of submission make your skin crawl? Does the word immediately create a vision in your mind of being trampled on like a doormat? Do you find being called a "helper" offensive? Our past experiences, along with voices from the world around us, can tempt us to think this way. And yet, in one of God's great paradoxes, he teaches us that we are most liberated when we understand that our role as a woman is as a helper. Personally, I never struggle with submission . . . as long as everyone else agrees with me and thinks the same way I think! Now when other people disagree or think differently than me . . . that's a different story altogether. How about you?

A Helper Suitable

When you think of the expression "the help," what do you think of? Most often, we think of someone hired to do a job we don't want to do or have time to do. In the movie *The Help,* a maid named

Aibileen repeated a mantra to the young girl in her care, a saying that helped shape the little girl's thinking: "You is kind. You is smart. You is important." Aibileen (the help) knew that even though the little girl was privileged and "free," she desperately needed to know her true identity and value.

More importantly, God has sent a message to us as women about his love for us, his purpose for us, and our precious value in his sight. God demonstrated his love and our value even in the way he created us.

> The LORD God said, "It is not good for the man to be alone. I will make a helper suitable for him." Now the LORD God had formed out of the ground all the beasts of the field and all the birds of the air. He brought them to the man to see what he would name them; and whatever the man called each living creature, that was its name. So the man gave names to all the livestock, the birds of the air and all the beasts of the field. But for Adam no suitable helper was found. So the LORD God caused the man to fall into a deep sleep; and while he was sleeping, he took one of the man's ribs and closed up the place with flesh. Then the LORD God made a woman from the rib he had taken out of the man, and he brought her to the man. Genesis 2:18–22

> So God created man in his own image, **in the image of God** he created him; male and female, **he created them.** Genesis 1:27 (emphasis added)

Carefully and Purposefully Created

Even though God created women later than men, we were not an afterthought. (Ever heard the phrase, "He saved the best for last"?) The animals had already been created as male and female, but God chose to create the female human at a later time. Perhaps God timed Eve's creation so that Adam could have a little time alone and come to understand that he was incomplete without her! The animals were simply not enough to keep him company. I would imagine that Adam soon learned that the porcupine was not pleasant to hug, and the aroma of the skunk was not pleasing to his olfactory senses. Have you ever seen a perfume called "eau de skunk"? I think not. The warthog's beauty left something to be desired, and the call of the loon was rather haunting. Adam needed a true companion with whom he could converse, share emotions, and share love—someone designed in God's image.

Whatever his reasons, God knew that creation was incomplete until woman was formed. Women were uniquely fashioned by God with plan and forethought. There are several different Hebrew words for "create" or "make" in the Genesis 2 account of the creation of woman. The word used for the creation of man translates as "formed." The word used for the creation of woman has a subtle difference in meaning—it is better translated as "fashioned" or "built," much like an architect plans and constructs a building, or as an artist plans and designs a work of art.[3]

From the very beginning of creation, God designed woman to be a suitable helpmeet for man. Eve was given an identity and purpose from the beginning—as Adam's helper. As we take a closer look at the term "helper," I hope you will gain a new view and a new respect for what it means to be "the help."

Being a helper is not a second-rate or inferior position, but rather it is an identity and a role—an important role. A helper is defined as someone suitable and complementary. The position carries with it a sense of urgency and of nurturing.

God specifically designed woman with qualities and characteristics that make her a complement, a corresponding part to man. God provided her with the physical, emotional, and cognitive abilities to fulfill her role as a helpmeet. Genesis 2 says that Eve was perfectly designed to fill a role that no one else in all creation could fill. She was suited to fill in Adam's gaps, to do and to be all that he could not do and be.

God Is Our Helper.

Women are in good company in our role as helpers—divine company! God himself is a helper—*our* helper. Amazingly, the same word for *helper* in Genesis 2 verses 18 and 20 is used in the following verses to describe God:

> There is no one like God of Jeshurun, who rides across the heavens **to help** you and on the clouds in majesty. Deuteronomy 33:26 (emphasis added)

> Blessed are you, Israel! Who is like you, a people saved by the Lord? He is your shield and **helper** and your glorious sword. Deuteronomy 33:29 (emphasis added)

> We wait in hope for the Lord; he is our **help** and shield. Psalm 33:20 (emphasis added)

> So we say with confidence, "The Lord is my **helper**; I will not be afraid. What can man do to me?" Hebrews 13:6 (emphasis added)

"Helper" is our God-given identity as women—whether we are single, married, single mothers, or widowed. Helping is not for the weak or faint of heart. When we as women accept this role from God, we become living vessels to demonstrate God's character and his heart to others. We reflect his image.

When God created woman, he endowed her with value and purpose. It was as if he, as *our* helper, bent down to us and said, "You is kind. You is smart. You is important." Or maybe he said, "You are beautiful, you are intelligent, you are valued, and you are mine."

Will you believe God and renew your thinking about being "the help?"

Jesus Went First.

If you still think a position as a helper is an insulting status meant only for weak or inferior people, consider that Jesus also lived a life of submission. Hebrews 5:7–8 shows us that Jesus, the agent of creation, the Son of God, King of kings and Lord of lords, submitted himself to the Father.

In Ephesians 5:22–30, we see the order that God has established in marriage; such submission is also a beautiful reflection of Jesus and the church. Wives are commanded to submit to their husbands. Husbands are commanded to love their wives sacrificially, as Christ loves the church and gave himself up for her. Which is harder? The truth is, both commands present challenges, and Jesus' example shows us how to fulfill both roles. Is this how you understand submission? Is this how you live it? Submission recognizes our dependence upon one another (Ephesians 4:15–16). We are taught to submit to one another (Ephesians 5:21); to submit to governing authorities (Romans 13:1); and to leaders in the church (Hebrews 13:17). Submission takes great strength of character, combined with humility.

Jesus, the son of God, showed us the strength required in godly submission, as Philippians 2:3–11 so beautifully describes:

> Do nothing out of selfish ambition or vain conceit, but in humility consider others better than yourselves. Each of you should look not

only to your own interests, but also to the interests of others.

Your attitude should be the same as that of
 Christ Jesus:

Who, being in very nature God,
 did not consider equality with God something to be grasped,
but made himself nothing,
 taking the very nature of a servant,
 being made in human likeness.
And being found in appearance as a man,
 he humbled himself
 and became obedient to death—even
 death on a cross!
Therefore God exalted him to the highest
 place
 and gave him the name that is above every
 name,
that at the name of Jesus every knee should
 bow,
 in heaven and on earth and under the
 earth,
and every tongue confess that Jesus Christ
 is Lord,
 to the glory of God the Father."

When the Scriptures call for women to be submissive to our husbands in 1 Peter 3, the verse begins with the sentence, "Wives, in the same way be
submissive to your husbands." The phrase "in the
same way" refers to the example of Jesus on the
cross as described in 1 Peter 2—on the cross, Jesus

"entrusted himself to him who judges justly." He did not retaliate. In his death and in his life, Jesus shows us how to have this strength of submission. He, as our helper, gives us the strength and example to become a helper.

Accepting God's Plan

Accepting God's plan for our life takes humility. It means we believe our Creator knows best how we are meant to function. However, Satan tries again and again to deceive us and to tempt us to think differently. He wants us to believe that God does not value us or have our best interests in mind.

What is the truth about submission? Submission is placing one's self under the authority or rank of another, and it is something we all are required to do—not just in marriage, but in other relationships as well. Submission begins with surrendering to God—obeying his commands and living according to his plans. It means we are not resisting or fighting God. Everyone (male *and* female) who seeks a relationship with God must surrender and live in submission to God's authority. Submission is not a position of weakness; rather, as the following scriptures show, submission takes humility, courage, and strength:

> And what does the LORD require of you?
> To act justly and to love mercy
>   and to walk humbly with your God.
> Micah 6:8

> Jesus said to them all, "If anyone would come after me, he must deny himself and take up his cross daily and follow me." Luke 9:23

> "You are my friends if you do what I command." John 15:14

A Helper to Your Husband

You may be saying to yourself, "Okay, sure I can submit to God. He's perfect—he's *God*. No problem there. But submit to men? Submit to my *husband?* (Have you *met* my husband?) Forget it!" It's one thing to submit to a perfect and loving God; it's another thing to submit to an imperfect human—and for many women, submitting to a *man* is a terrifying prospect. Certainly men who are not following God's plan have played a part in planting such doubts in our hearts.

Ever since the Garden, male-female relationships have been orchestrated and manipulated by Satan to encourage women to reject and fear the concept of submission. We can find countless examples of ways that men have demeaned women through history—treating them as property, as inferior, as unintelligent, as sex symbols, and the list goes on. Whenever this happens, wherever it happens, God's plan for man and woman becomes twisted and distorted, and God is grieved.

But the truth is, submission—particularly submission in the marriage relationship—was a tough concept for women from the beginning, starting with the very first couple, and with Satan's encounter with Eve. In fact, the ongoing struggle between the genders seems to be one consequence of Eve's sin, as we see in Genesis 3:16:

> To the woman [God] said,
> "I will greatly increase your pains in
>   childbearing;
>   with pain you will give birth to children.
> Your **desire** will be for your husband,
>   and he will rule over you."
> Genesis 3:16 (emphasis added)

I did not understand this until reading further in Genesis 4:6–7, which says,

> "Then the LORD said to Cain, 'Why are you angry? Why is your face downcast? If you do what is right, will you not be accepted? But if you do not do what is right, sin is crouching at your door; it **desires** to have you, but you must master it.' " Genesis 4:6–7 (emphasis added)

The word *desire* has the same meaning in both passages. When we read, "Your desire will be for your husband" and "sin . . . desires to have you," it is clear that in both places the word *desire* has to do with the desire for control. Just as sin crouching at Cain's door desired to control or to master him, so also women, through the curse handed down to us through Eve, desire to take control over our husbands—even though God has placed the husband as the authority in marriage.

"What?" you may be thinking. "Does this mean I have to live my life being stifled under a man's authority?" We all must come to understand that when God's plan is carried out as he intended—forged with love, respect, humility, and with an understanding of the tremendous value God places on women—submission is freeing, not stifling. (Please note: There may be instances where one could confusion submission with enabling abusive conduct. The laws of our land protect us from oppressive behavior and there are times a woman may need to remove herself, or someone else, from a particular situation in order to be safe from harm.) When men and women are both fulfilling their God-ordained roles with proper love, respect, and appreciation for each other, both genders feel fulfilled, secure, and confident.

And consider this: Submission is about *order*, not *importance*. Creation was ordered. The sun came before the earth and animals and humans. Is the sun most important? No—but it provided what the rest of creation needed in order to thrive. Order is always needed for harmony in physics, in science, and in relationships. It has been crafted by God. And when it comes to the ordering of relationships, the goal of submission is to work together as one to accomplish God's purpose (see Galatians 3:28; 1 Corinthians 12:14–20).

If I'm Single, Who Am I Supposed to Help?

You may be wondering, if you are single, how submission applies to you. Our God-given role as a "helper" is universal—whether we are married or single. Outside the marriage relationship, it translates into a godly attitude and a gracious frame of mind. Being a woman does not mean that we are unable to serve as managers or leaders at work or in other settings; but it does influence the way we interact with the men around us. We are all called to an attitude of respect, kindness, and courtesy—not competition.

Our attitudes toward our brothers in Christ, coworkers, church leaders, employers, and employees convey either respect or disrespect. Married or single, we can "roll our eyes" (even in our minds) or speak in condescending ways, as if we "know it all." Some of us treat men as though they are our children, or are young boys. This does not show respect. We can also be quick to speak and slow to listen, which shows that we respect ourselves more than others.

I know many strong women (single and married) in various professions and stages of life who choose to gracefully show respect to the people around them—including men who they oversee or manage in their jobs. This respectful, submissive attitude shows up in a woman's body language, her words to and about others, and ultimately in the way she thinks as she relates to people.

I have known other women who seem to need to prove they are "in control." They would rather throw themselves overboard than consider themselves a "helper" to anyone—particularly to a man. Armed with short tempers, bossy demeanors, rude tones, and "put-downs," they emotionally castrate the men around them.

A woman's acceptance of God's role for her life is evident in the confident grace she exudes; this humble confidence results when she knows that she is loved by God and is his precious and chosen possession. Then, and only then, does she feel secure, free from the need to prove herself to anyone (including herself). She accepts God's role for her life and is comfortable and free in embracing her role as "helper."

Trusting God as Our Helper

I am brought to tears of gratitude when I think about how God has stooped down as my helper. Great as he is, he has humbled himself to draw near to me, listen to me, and be my Father and friend:

> He reached down from on high and took hold
> of me;
>   he drew me out of deep waters.
> He rescued me from my powerful enemy,
>   from my foes, who were too strong for me.
> They confronted me in the day of my
>   disaster,

but the LORD was my support.
He brought me out into a spacious place;
he rescued me because he delighted in
me. Psalm 18:16–19

God is our helper. We are created in his image and he delights in us. He asks nothing of us that he has not first demonstrated. He always goes first. "We love, because he first loved us" (1 John 4:19).

We can learn to be helpers, because God has shown us how. I pray we all trust him in the process of learning to live freely under authority. As we grow in our role as helpers, let us remember that God has promised us, "You are kind, you are beautiful, you are smart, and you are mine."

Taking It Deeper:

Am I Really the Help?

Reflect on God's intentions for submission and consider the following two treaties below: One shows submission, and one does not. Which one would you find easier to sign? If you tend to offer God the terms of your surrender, decide one thing you will do from this point forward to overcome your fear of surrendering to him.

Treaty of Surrender #1

I do hereby surrender control of my life to my Lord and Creator, under the following conditions and terms:

1. _____

2. _____

3. _____

(Attach additional pages as needed.)

_____

Your name

Treaty of Surrender #2

I do hereby surrender control of my life to my Lord and Creator.

_____

Your name

Chapter 4

Overcoming Fear

Since God has lovingly designed us with significance and purpose, why is it so scary to place ourselves in a posture of submission to him and to others? Whether we are young or old, married or single, rich or poor, we often fight to find faith when our fears raise their ugly heads. Fear can have a powerful hold on us.

It became obvious early on that I would struggle with fear my whole life. In kindergarten, I ran away from school and hid in our garage because I had forgotten my lunch money. (I guess I thought I'd be put in some sort of principal's jail!) I was unconsciously following Eve's example—she also hid in fear. And still today, my imagination can quickly kick into action. If I can't reach a family member, I begin to imagine them in all sorts of frightening scenarios.

I am also desperately afraid of heights. I can't stand to be high up or even to watch other people who are up high, especially if they are near an edge—just watching makes my heart feel like it has sunk into my feet. I have to hold myself back when

I go to our local mall and see other people's children go anywhere near the five-foot tall, steel-reinforced glass wall that serves as a safety barrier between the second floor and the ground level. I have an overwhelming urge to scoop them up and carry them somewhere away from the very scary glass—after all, what if the child touched it, and the glass fell over? What if the child was able to scale the wall? I can just envision mall security arresting me for picking up someone else's child!

Thankfully, God knows we are tempted with fear. Women are prone to being fearful, and God specifically speaks to us about it. In 1 Peter 3, he calls us to imitate Sarah and the way she overcame fear in submitting both to her husband and to God's plan for her life. God says, "You are her daughters if you do what is right and do not give way to fear" (1 Peter 3:6).

Fear or Faith

Fear and faith can't coexist for long. One will overrule the other. Fear, from faithlessness, is sparked by Satan and is the fuel he uses to consume our faith as he tries to destroy our relationship with God; he implants doubts about God's true character and intentions for us.

Paradoxically, faith is the fuel through which God can work in our lives. God clearly defines the role of faith in overcoming fear. The Bible gives numerous examples of people whose faith vanquished their fear—along with examples of fear overcoming faith.

Hebrews 11 opens with accounts of men and women who lived "by faith"; but all too often our faithless mindset could write another chapter that begins with the words, "By fear . . ."

A chapter written about me in my faithless moments might read, "By fear...

By fear, Jeanie woke up thinking that since things were going well in her life, God must be preparing something bad for her. Therefore she became anxious.

By fear, Jeanie gave up on trying to have an honest and spiritual relationship with a friend who disappointed her, because she assumed that things could never change.

By fear, Jeanie did not share her faith with the woman standing next to her in the grocery line. Jeanie stood behind her, thoughts racing: Why would a woman who was busy fighting with her husband on the phone be interested in hearing about a God who can heal relationships?

This chapter could go on and on! How might this chapter read in your life? What are some of the things you fear? Many women fear not having control over situations in their lives. Many of us believe that we alone know what is best for our life, and we can't trust anyone else with our life—not even our Creator. This is one of Satan's lies. God is fully capable of taking care of our needs and guiding us in the direction we need to go.

What Do We Fear?

We can fear God's motives. We can think that God does not have good intentions for us, that he does not love us, or that he is out to punish us or "get us." Yet the Bible, which is the truth from God, tells us that God loved us so much that he gave his Son to die for us (John 3:16). If God made the supreme sacrifice of his Son, why would he not give us whatever else we need? (Romans 8:32) We read in 2 Peter 1:3–4 that God will give us everything we need for life and godliness.

Just yesterday, one of my good friends, a woman who was younger than me, died of a terrible disease similar to ALS. Her mind stayed sharp while her body wasted away. Today I learned that another dear friend's husband has an advanced aggressive cancer that has spread throughout his body. Things like this can seem unfair, and tempt me to fear that God has forgotten his people. I can be tempted to fear that someone else I love is next. Faith tells me to remember that God is always able to work his good will in those who are called according to his purpose (Romans 8:28). God kept Adam and Eve from eating from the tree that would cause them to live forever, and so none of us are promised tomorrow. However, we are promised eternal life (John 11:25–26) and cautioned not to fear those who can kill the body but cannot kill the soul:

> "Do not be afraid of those who kill the body but cannot kill the soul. Rather, be afraid of

> the One who can destroy both soul and body in hell. Are not two sparrows sold for a penny? Yet not one of them will fall to the ground apart from the will of your Father. And even the very hairs of your head are all numbered. So don't be afraid; you are worth more than many sparrows." Matthew 10:28–31

We often fear the opinions and judgments of other people, which is a form of giving in to peer pressure. We can become consumed with what others will think of us, or what will they say to us or about us. We fear they won't accept us. When we do this, we consider other people and their opinions more valuable than God's truth and our relationship with him.

We may also fear a loss of personal comfort when we are called to sacrifice of our time, money, or convenience.

We might fear anonymity and not being acknowledged. This leads us to feeling unimportant, unloved, and taken for granted, and we become even more insecure. We've all known people (or *been* people!) who appear confident and well put-together, but have an insatiable need to be acknowledged, thanked, and reassured. This kind of "need" comes from deep-seated fears and insecurities.

Or we might fear being acknowledged, because then we feel pressured to live up to others' expectations of us. Those of us who tend toward perfectionism may fear being open with our failures—we worry about messing up and disappointing people (including—and perhaps especially—ourselves).

We may fear being taken advantage of or being mistreated or abused. It is normal to fear these things, especially if we have experienced abusive situations. It is important to remember that abuse comes from Satan's work in people's lives causing evil—not from God. Abuse grieves God. We need to recall the truth about God—that he is light and in him there is no darkness (1 John 1:5). God is light and love. Abuse comes from darkness. Remember the great care with which God created woman, and the high calling he gave us. This has not changed because of Satan's work in others' lives.

Jesus' View of Women

We can be tempted to think that God gave us our role because he thinks less of us than he thinks of men. But that is another of Satan's lies. A different *role* does not mean a different *value*. Jesus, whose job was to model God's love here on earth, clearly demonstrated God's respect and love for women. Jesus continually shocked his contemporaries by reinterpreting the cultural norms of the day in his relationships with women. Sometimes we miss the cultural significance of the things Jesus did, because our modern culture and perspective are so different—but when it came to his treatment of women, Jesus was a revolutionary. Time and again he crossed cultural and traditional norms in order to demonstrate God's love, appreciation, and respect for women—and to call others to follow in his example. Lest we think that God slighted women, take note of some of Jesus' interactions with women.

Consider the woman at the well, whose story unfolds in John 4. Jesus chose her—a woman—as the first person in Samaria to whom he disclosed his divinity. In John 8, Jesus showed compassion to a "sinful woman" to teach a group of men. Jesus had many women friends who played special roles in his ministry. Mary and Martha were his friends and were engaged in his ministry (Luke 10), along with Mary Magdalene, Salome, Mary the mother of James and Joseph, and others. And Jesus chose to make his first resurrection appearance to a group of these women (Mark 16:1–10).

> You are all sons of God through faith in Christ Jesus, for all of you who were baptized into Christ have clothed yourselves with Christ. There is neither Jew nor Greek, slave nor free, male nor female, for you are all one in Christ Jesus. If you belong to Christ, then you are Abraham's seed, and heirs according to the promise. Galatians 3:26–29

Paul's words mean that a woman's standing before God was (and is) one of complete equality. This stood in stark contrast to first-century society's lowly view of women. Romans 16 gives us numerous examples of women who served in the church and perhaps were even supported financially for their service to the church.

God values women. He sent his Son to die in order to show us how much. We don't always understand his methods—his ways are not our ways, and his thoughts are not our thoughts (Isaiah 55:8–9)—but God promises that he always has our best interests in mind.

> "Which of you, if his son asks for bread, will give him a stone? Or if he asks for a fish, will give him a snake? If you, then, though you are evil, know how to give good gifts to your children, how much more will your Father in heaven give good gifts to those who ask him!"
> Matthew 7:9–11

As mothers, we would never consider ways to hurt our children, even though we are imperfect parents. In the same way, God (our heavenly parent) is perfect and always has our good in mind.

When I struggle with fear (which unfortunately is too often) I look to scriptures such as these to strengthen my faith:

> The LORD is my light and my salvation—
>   whom shall I fear?
> The LORD is the stronghold of my life—
>   of whom shall I be afraid? Psalm 27:1
>
> Though an army besiege me,
>   my heart will not fear;
> though war break out against me,
>   even then will I be confident. Psalm 27:3

When we have complete awe and respect for God— "right kind of fear"—we are able to understand that nothing is too big or small for him to handle.

> The fear of the LORD is the beginning of
> > wisdom;
> > all who follow his precepts have good
> > understanding.
> > To him belongs eternal praise.
> Psalm 111:10

> He will have no fear of bad news;
> > his heart is steadfast, trusting in the LORD.
> His heart is secure, he will have no fear;
> > in the end he will look in triumph on his
> > > foes. Psalm 112:7–8

> You who fear him, trust in the LORD—
> > he is their help and shield. Psalm 115:11

> "So do not fear, for I am with you;
> > do not be dismayed, for I am your God.
> I will strengthen you and help you;
> > I will uphold you with my righteous right
> > > hand." Isaiah 41:10

> For I am the LORD, your God,
> > who takes hold of your right hand
> and says to you, Do not fear;
> > I will help you. Isaiah 41:13

> But now, this is what the LORD says—
> > he who created you, O Jacob,
> > he who formed you, O Israel:

"Fear not, for I have redeemed you;
   I have summoned you by name; you are
     mine." Isaiah 43:1

Over and over, God reassures us that he is with us, he is for us, and he is watching us. We can trust him with our lives, our hopes, and our happiness.

Overcoming Fear

Scripture verifies the love and value God has for women. Every day we must choose to believe the truth about his love for us. Overcoming our fears requires us to step out on faith, taking one step at a time. You and I can choose to change what could be written about our fears in our own personal "fearful rendition" of Hebrews 11. As for me, I can decide to trust God's love and intention for good in my life, thus allowing faith to triumph over fear.

In a difficult relationship, I can choose to have the faith to follow Jesus in his example of unconditional love. Then, as 1 Corinthians 13 tells me, I can have the faith to protect, trust, hope, and persevere. When I believe that the fields are ripe for harvest, as God tells me they are (John 4:35), I can overcome my fears and share my faith with the distracted women in line next to me. Let us all tackle our fears and begin to live our lives as Hebrews 11 actually states: by faith.

Taking It Deeper:

Overcoming Fear

I encourage you to overcome your fear one step at a time. Keep it simple—make one decision at a time. Here are some practical things you can do to strengthen your faith and overcome fear:

1. Focus your attention on God and life with him (Colossians 3:1–3).

2. Read the following helpful scriptures to understand that God is trustworthy.

   • Psalm 27:1

   • Psalm 73:21–26

   • Psalm 36:5–6

   • Psalm 89:14

   • Psalm 92:4

   • Lamentations 3:22–24

   • Hebrews 10:19–24

3. Memorize scriptures that encourage your faith, or keep them handy as a ready reference.

4. Pray for God's perspective: Pray that God will change your vision, that he will help you to see yourself and others the way he does. Study the following applicable passages:

   • Proverbs 14:12

   • Philippians 4:8

   • Hebrews 12:2

5. Find trustworthy people to share your fears with. Pray with them and ask them to pray for you.

6. Write down some ways you might overcome your fear of surrendering to God's will. Take time to share your ideas with others.

Chapter 5

The Freedom of Forgiveness

Have you ever felt weighed down by bitter thoughts toward someone? Do past events, especially times when you experienced hurt or disappointment, keep traveling through your mind? Bitterness takes over when forgiveness doesn't happen. Anger, pain, and disappointment can take root in our hearts, impact the way we interpret all interactions in our life, and bloom into the destructive weed of bitterness. Bitterness is a lack of forgiveness stretched over time. Bitterness destroys. Have you ever met a bitter person who is free and happy? I haven't.

What Does Bitterness Look Like?

How can we know if we are bitter? There is no better place to look than the Bible. The Scriptures always help us see ourselves clearly. In Proverbs 5:4, bitterness is described as "gall." When we are locked up with bitterness, we understand this comparison. Bitterness feels like bitter stomach acid that eats us up inside. Bitterness, and the emotions that accompany it, are like that acid—they can even affect our physical health.

Proverbs 14:10 states that each heart knows its own bitterness, and no one else can share its joy. This can be seen in many practical ways.

- We become "alone in our own head." Feeling isolated, we won't let anyone into our hearts for fear of receiving more pain. We become unhappy, discontent and critical—unable to be cheered by others.

- Our words reflect the hurt, pain and resentment we hold inside. Romans 3:14 says, "Their mouths are full of cursing and bitterness." Our words become evidence of our bitterness.

- Bitterness is graceless. We miss the grace of God when we harbor anger and resentment. When we are bitter, we don't feel God's grace, we don't give it to others, and we don't enjoy it ourselves. We miss it altogether. The Scriptures speak in strong terms about this, calling us to "see to it" that no one misses the grace of God. We must help each other when we see bitterness creeping into our hearts.

  See to it that no one misses the grace of God and that no bitter root grows up to cause trouble and defile many. Hebrews 12:15

Bitterness is a sin that invites and nurtures company. It always brings its cousins (rage, anger, brawling, and every form of malice) to its party.

> Get rid of all bitterness, rage and anger, brawling and slander, along with every form of malice. Ephesians 4:31

Where Does Bitterness Come From?

I have found that it's difficult to change something when we don't know what it is we need to change. We assume that our experiences make us the way we are. We think, "I am this way because something happened to me, or someone did something to me, or I grew up a certain way. I can't help it. This is the way I am doomed to think, and act, and feel, and be, for the rest of my life. There's nothing I can do to be different."

Consider carefully this question: Do hurts, disappointments, and abusive or unfair treatment *make* us bitter, or do they *tempt* us to be bitter? There is a crucial difference between these two options.

Absolutely no one can force us to be bitter. You are the only one who can determine how you will respond to hurt. Sinful thoughts (including bitterness) come from inside our own hearts. They are not caused by things done to us. If we don't accept this truth, we will always remain a victim of other people's sin, and Satan will win twice—once with the people who sinned against us, and a second time with our sinful response.

> "For from within, out of men's hearts, come evil thoughts, sexual immorality, theft, murder, adultery, greed, malice, deceit, lewdness, envy, slander, arrogance and folly. All these evils come from inside and make a man 'unclean.' " Mark. 7:21–23

Sinful thinking comes not from the circumstances surrounding us, but from our hearts within us.

Because we are responsible for our responses, the good news is that we have power over our reactions to hurt and pain, and over the bitterness that can take root in our hearts. Because of this, *we can decide* to repent and overcome, which is such a freeing process, since bitterness only hurts and destroys.

Who Does Bitterness Hurt?

Sometimes we don't *want* to leave our hurts and go to a place of complete forgiveness. We may think it is too difficult, or maybe we think it would be unfair to let it go—after all, someone needs to pay! Meanwhile, the other person who hurt us goes on about their merry way, and *we* pay the price. Resentment, anger, and bitterness take their toll on our character, attitudes, and interactions. Meanwhile, we hurt ourselves, we hurt God, and we hurt people around us—often those we love the most.

You may be thinking, *Really? My bitterness also hurts God?* Bitterness grieves our Father, as we read in Ephesians 4 and in other passages:

> And do not grieve the Holy Spirit of God, with
> whom you were sealed for the day of re-
> demption. Get rid of all bitterness, rage and
> anger, brawling and slander, along with every
> form of malice. Ephesians 4:30–31

As we read about God's response to Eve in earlier chapters, this scripture also reminds us that the God of the universe cares and feels for us. This amazes me and touches my soul.

Bitterness in our heart, along with its terrible relatives—anger, malice and slander— spreads like a toxic fume and affects our family, friends, and coworkers. It grows up and oozes out of us, hurting and defiling everyone around us (Hebrews 12:15).

Lack of forgiveness hurts *us* as well. When we don't forgive, we miss God's grace and are left unforgiven. This is not a good place to stay. Not only are we in an unforgiven state, but we are eaten up from the inside by the gall of bitterness. Jesus warns us, "For if you forgive men when they sin against you, your heavenly Father will also forgive you. But if you do not forgive men their sins, your Father will not forgive your sins" (Matthew 6:14–15).

Thankfully, since we are responsible for our hearts, we can choose to break free from this heavy load and vicious cycle, and to find and feel the true freedom and internal peace that come from complete forgiveness.

Freedom of Forgiveness

Being set free from bitterness and coming to a place of forgiveness will take time and effort. Here are some crucial steps to take as you begin this journey.

1. Identify the source of your pain.

Sometimes we don't realize that we are shackled with "undealt with" pain. As a result, we may feel "displaced anger"—anger that pops up in the wrong places, toward the wrong people. We can find ourselves "flying off the handle" with our family and friends. We can become disagreeable, critical, and judgmental. We can have an underlying sense of anxiety and even depression. We can feel worthless and angry at ourselves—even to the point of inflicting pain on ourselves.

One of my friends, "Jane," had deep periods of sadness and self-loathing, and sometimes she cut herself as a result of her displaced pain. As we talked together about her life, I asked her if she had been hurt in her past. She responded that her life seemed pretty normal to her, although she had gone through some difficult things. As I asked her to share some of the tough things she had experienced, she told me that her older brother had raped her almost daily, beginning when she was just four years old. All of her life, she had surmised that it was she who had done wrong, and she placed no blame on her brother, whom she loved.

As we talked, cried, read scriptures, and prayed, I tried to help her see how deeply her brother had hurt her and robbed her of her childhood. He had done evil to her and sinned grievously against her. His actions had affected nearly every aspect of her life. It was quite difficult for her to place blame on anyone but herself for his evil deeds. Eventually, as she thought and prayed about it and allowed herself to "go there," she came to the realization that he had sinned terribly against her. It was extremely important for her to identify the source of the pain that had caused her so much grief. Once she had done this, she was able to move forward and eventually reach forgiveness. If we can't identify the source, we won't be able to specifically forgive someone. We won't find that place of forgiveness— and freedom.

It's important to note that the things I'm sharing here are not easy to do. Revisiting pain is hard work, but it will be worth it, if it leads to a place of forgiveness and healing. I encourage you, if you have deep-seated issues in your past from abuse, please seek wise counsel from sisters in Christ, so you don't go through this alone. You will need support.

2. Allow yourself to "feel the hurt."

As hard as this is, it's important to let ourselves feel the pain we should feel when someone or something has hurt us. If we don't let ourselves feel the pain, we will most likely stuff the associated feelings deep inside—and as a result we will close off our emotions and become hardened. Although our emotions may be tightly closed in, they will find their way out when we don't expect it or desire it. Smells, places, words, or tones of voice can spark a memory, hijack our minds, and send us into dark places of hopelessness and grief. When we have not allowed ourselves to feel and "deal with" the pain we have experienced, our hidden emotions can surprise us and sometimes overtake us. If we don't take the time to deal with our hurt, or even the anger that follows it, we often won't be able to truly forgive. How can we forgive someone when we don't hold them responsible for anything?

When we go back to the Garden of Eden, we see God identify of the source of the pain that came from Eve's sin. God asked, "Who did this?" There was a clear assessment of responsibility for sin.

3. Confront that which is unresolved.

The Scriptures teach us to "go to" or confront the one who has hurt us. Often, we would rather go to the ends of the earth than do this. Fear most often keeps us from going to the person. We are tempted to play out different scenarios in our mind of what could happen, and then we are afraid to take the next step. It takes faith to deal with conflicts and grievances God's way.

While Matthew 18 is specifically talking about resolving conflict with a fellow Christian, by following the process of directly going to the person who has hurt us, we can find the freedom that comes with forgiveness:

> "If your brother sins against you, go and show him his fault, just between the two of you. If he listens to you, you have won your brother over. But if he will not listen, take one or two others along, so that 'every matter may be established by the testimony of two or three witnesses.' If he refuses to listen to them, tell it to the church; and if he refuses to listen even to the church, treat him as you would a pagan or a tax collector." Matthew 18:15–17

4. Offer forgiveness.

This step takes prayer, wisdom, and discretion. We must first decide that we WILL offer forgiveness, and forgive from our heart—no matter how the other person responds. This is crucial. Remember, *we* are the only ones responsible for what we hold in our hearts. No one else can be held responsible for *our* response.

Ideally, it is best to speak directly to the person. If for some reason it is unwise to go directly to the person (for example, if they are unstable or dangerous), or if the person is not available or is no longer living, you can write a letter to them. In your letter, it is important to tell the person what happened and how it affected (and still affects) you. Be real and don't hold back the truth. (They need to hear this. This process may also open a door for them to get the help they need to change.)

Remember, don't worry about how they are going to respond. Right now, this is about you finding forgiveness in your heart. You can't be responsible for the other person's reaction. You must do your part. They will have to do theirs.

It takes work, decision, courage, and faith to get to the place where you can truly forgive. You must always have faith that God's way is right. Your actions and feelings can't be dependent on whether or not someone else takes responsibility for their sins. Finding the freedom in forgiveness is about *our* hearts and the way *we* respond to people and to our past.

We can only get to this place of true forgiveness by holding to Jesus' example of forgiveness. The basis of all forgiveness is the cross of Christ. Let us always remember Jesus' words of forgiveness for his murderers, even as he hung on the cross, suffering and dying: "Father, forgive them, for they do not know what they are doing" (Luke 23:34).

I have often wondered if the most challenging temptation Jesus ever faced was bitterness. Satan could have won the battle at the end of Jesus' life, even while Jesus was on the cross—perhaps Jesus' greatest temptation to sin came as he was dying. I can only imagine how tempting it would have been to become bitter, while hanging there looking out at those he had given his life for, but who were now spitting in his face and mocking him. In my mind, he would have every right to be angry, to show them who he was and to wipe them out. He had loved them and sacrificed everything for them. He was about to experience separation from his Father. The physical and emotional pain were unimaginable, and yet he did not succumb to the temptation to be bitter. I wonder if he said "Father forgive them" for *his* own sake—to banish bitterness from his heart.

What Does Forgiveness Look Like?

What does forgiveness look like? How do you know if you have truly forgiven someone? It is always most helpful find answers through scriptures. Numerous passages about God's grace show us what forgiveness looks like.

> As far as the east is from the west,
>> so far has he removed our transgressions
>>> from us. Psalm 103:12

> "No longer will a man teach his neighbor,
>> or a man his brother, saying, 'Know the
>>> Lord,'
> because they will all know me,
>> from the least of them to the greatest,"
>>> declares the Lord.
> "For I will forgive their wickedness
>> and will remember their sins no more."
> Jeremiah 31:34

> Love is patient, love is kind. It does not envy, it does not boast, it is not proud. It is not rude, it is not self-seeking, it is not easily angered, it keeps no record of wrongs. Love does not delight in evil but rejoices with the truth. It always protects, always trusts, always hopes, always perseveres. 1 Corinthians 13:4–7

When we forgive people who have offended us, our former grievances and all their associated feelings don't keep coming up in our minds. We truly let them go and don't remember them.

You may wonder how you can get to this point. It may seem impossible! If that's how you feel, you are in good company.

Consider the apostles' response to Jesus' teaching on forgiveness:

> "So watch yourselves. If your brother sins, rebuke him, and if he repents, forgive him. If he sins against you seven times in a day, and seven times comes back to you and says, 'I repent,' forgive him."
>
> The apostles said to the Lord, **"Increase our faith!"** Luke 17:3–5 (emphasis added)

How Do We Let Things Go?

1. No strings attached.

It takes great faith to forgive. We may at times muster up the courage to confront someone who has hurt us, but still hold on to an idea of how we think the conversation should go before we will fully forgive. We think that if he or she says "this," then we'll say "that." But if they don't "get it," we aren't willing to move on.

2. Wash, Rinse, Repeat.

Sometimes, we think we have forgiven someone, and then the person does something again that brings up the same old feelings—and we throw our hands up in dismay, thinking we can't go any further in forgiving. Remember that forgiveness does not happen only once—forgiveness must be offered time and time again—sometimes daily! In Matthew 18, Jesus explains this idea to Peter:

> Then Peter came to Jesus and asked, "Lord, how many times shall I forgive my brother when he sins against me? Up to seven times?"
> Jesus answered, "I tell you, not seven times, but seventy-seven times." Matthew 18:21–22

When Jesus said seventy-seven times, he meant however many times it takes. He did not mean that on the seventy-eighth time we could be done with forgiving. Forgiveness has to keep going. God forgives each of us over and over and over again, and we should treat other people in the same way.

3. Trust that God will deal with the other person.

Remember Jesus' words, "Father forgive them, they don't know what they are doing." Like Jesus, we must learn obedience through trials and suffering, and entrust all situations to God, who judges justly. Even though we don't always see it, God is disciplining the other person in his own way, trying to bring them to a place of repentance.

> When they hurled their insults at him, he did not retaliate; when he suffered, he made no threats. Instead, **he entrusted himself to him who judges justly**. 1 Peter 2:23 (emphasis added)

Offering forgiveness and trusting God *doesn't* mean we do nothing. We must go through the process for our own healing to arrive at a place of true forgiveness.

4. Remember where you've come from.

In order to forgive, we must remember how much we have been forgiven by God. Matthew 18 continues with the parable of the unmerciful servant, who paid no mind to the mercy that had been shown him. At the end of the parable, Jesus says, "This is how my heavenly Father will treat each of you unless you forgive your brother from your heart" (Matthew 18:35).

> Bear with each other and forgive whatever grievances you may have against one another. Forgive as the Lord forgave you. Colossians 3:13

> "And when you stand praying, if you hold any-
> thing against anyone, forgive him, so that
> your Father in heaven may forgive you your
> sins." Mark 11:25

Emotions of Forgiveness

In the Bible, the account of Joseph is perhaps the most poignant example of forgiveness (except for Jesus). We can learn much from Joseph's example. Several standout lessons can be taken from Genesis 50:18–23, as Joseph offers forgiveness to his brothers. Out of jealousy, Joseph's brothers had sold him into slavery. From there, life didn't get any better—Joseph was falsely accused of rape and thrown into prison, where he was neglected and forgotten. Even after all that—a lifetime of loss and pain—Joseph still offered his brothers forgiveness. Verse 17 tells us that Joseph's father encouraged him to forgive, and Joseph wept when he received the message.

> His brothers then came and threw them-
> selves down before him. "We are your
> slaves," they said.
> But Joseph said to them, "Don't be afraid.
> Am I in the place of God? You intended to
> harm me, but God intended it for good to ac-
> complish what is now being done, the saving
> of many lives. So then, don't be afraid. I will
> provide for you and your children."
> And **he reassured them and spoke
> kindly to them**.

> Joseph stayed in Egypt, along with all his father's family. He lived a hundred and ten years and saw the third generation of Ephraim's children. Also the children of Makir son of Manasseh were placed at birth on Joseph's knees. Genesis 50:18–23 (emphasis added)

In verse 17 we see that Joseph's emotions flowed freely as he forgave. Relationships are renewed from the deep-seated emotions of our heart when we forgive. Verse 19 shows us that entrusting our situations to God can take away fear, just as the Scriptures promise—"perfect love drives out fear" (1 John 4:18).

In Genesis 50:20 we learn that even when people intentionally harm us, God in his sovereignty can take the bad and use it for good. In this he fulfills a promise made to us in Romans 8:28—that God works for the good of those who love him and who are called according to his purpose.

God grieves when sin abounds and we are hurt. We must be clear that sin is not from God but is from Satan, and all of mankind chooses to sin or not to sin. We are free agents. God is good, and even though evil and godlessness are everywhere, God can triumph through and over evil. Finally, in Genesis 50:21, we see that when there is true forgiveness, kind words and reassurance follow. Joseph reassured his brothers and spoke kindly to them.

Forgiveness is a beautiful thing. It adds health to your body, joy to your soul, and pep to your step. Most importantly, it restores relationships—with God, with others, and with yourself. In my years of counseling people, I have witnessed the powerful transformation that forgiveness brings. As they offer words of forgiveness, cry tears of joy, and offer long-overdue hugs, their entire demeanor changes. It is as if they have been let out of prison, or had heavy weights lifted from their shoulders. As I join in their tears (good tears!), I am reminded of this scene with Joseph and his brothers, and deeply grateful that God has shown us the way of forgiveness.

Determine if there is someone you have not forgiven from the heart. Have you decided whether or not you will be bitter and enslaved, or forgiving, forgiven, and free? Ask someone to pray with you and help you to break free. Take the steps outlined in this chapter. Don't give up. You can get there with the help and grace of God. God never asks us to do something he has not already done himself, and has not already empowered us to do.

Take bitterness by the roots and send it away, along with all of its horrible relatives. Lock the door behind them all. Once they are gone, you will begin to experience the uplifting joy and life-changing freedom that come from forgiveness.

Taking It Deeper:

Freedom of Forgiveness

Do you recognize yourself in either of these categories?

Bound by Bitterness

- I keep recounting the wrong someone did to me.

- I long for the one who hurt me to have to "pay," and/or I wish evil on them.

- I constantly blame myself and/or carry guilt for something I may or may not have done.

- I often talk negatively about the person(s) who hurt me.

- I find myself emotionally spiraling downward when I think about someone who has hurt me.

- I can't pray for the one who wronged me, as I wish nothing good for them.

- When I think of the person(s) who wronged me, I feel stressed and anxious.

- I don't want to let go of the pain that someone caused me. I will remain their victim; the hurt is just too great to let go.

Freed by Forgiveness

- I no longer keep track of another's wrongs toward me.

- What happens to someone else (who may have hurt me) no longer affects my joy, or lack thereof.

- I go to sleep at night with peace in my soul.

- I pray for those who have hurt me in the past.

- I no longer need to keep letting other people know how much someone hurt me.

- I have done all I can do to be resolved with the person who has hurt or wronged me. Although I may not yet be fully healed, I am resolved and I am at peace.

- Although I may not yet (or ever) trust the person who hurt me, I trust that God will deal with them and me according to his righteousness. This allows me to let go of my desire for control.

- I refuse to be a victim. I won't let another person control who I am or who I can become.

If you are still bound in bitterness, I encourage you to follow the steps outlined in chapter 5 to help you find forgiveness. Begin in prayer, asking God for his help, and by finding someone you trust to guide and encourage you through the process.

Chapter 6

Taking Every Thought Captive

As a child, on summer afternoons I often enjoyed the challenge of catching butterflies. I caught a few, but it wasn't easy using only my hands. Years later, when my children were young, I invested in a butterfly net, which made capturing them so much easier. The butterflies would flit and float from bush to bush. We would carefully put the net over them and then place them in a premade butterfly box, complete with leaves and flowers.

As women, our thoughts can be like these butterflies, flitting and floating from place to place. I can, in a mere instant, take an unfamiliar physical ailment and begin making arrangements for my family after my death. I can hear an inflection in someone's voice and determine that they are upset with me. I can second-guess each paragraph I write in this book and wonder how stupid it might sound . . . and ask myself why in the world I would attempt to write a book anyway. Our thoughts can wander even when we're trying to be spiritual. How many times have I started praying in my mind, and before I know it I'm thinking about the laundry and the appointments I have later in the day?

Can you relate? At times I have wondered, as I talk to other women, what their "thought bubbles" (the thoughts that are really going on behind their words, actions, smiles, and frowns) would say if I could read them.

God Knows Emotions.

Thankfully, God understands the range of emotions that can result from our thoughts and wild imaginings. He understands because he himself has emotions. His word teaches us that he loves, he grieves, he is a jealous God, he weeps, he rejoices, he is amazed, and he has felt anguish. God came to us in human form so he could identify with our every thought and emotion, and thus equip us to be victorious in our thought life.

Both psychology and physiology agree that our thoughts, feelings, and emotions are intimately connected. They can even affect our physical health. We don't always remember all the factual details of our experiences, but we do remember how they make us feel—and those feelings affect us in myriad ways. God knew long ago that our thought life influences our feelings and our health, and we see countless examples of this truth throughout Scripture.

We have already seen how Eve felt insecure and ashamed after she listened to Satan's lies. Later we see that Eve's son Cain was not obedient to God. This led to guilt, a downcast spirit, and anger:

> But on Cain and his offering [God] did not look with favor. So **Cain was very angry, and his face was downcast**.
>
> Then the LORD said to Cain, "Why are you angry? Why is your face downcast? If you do what is right, will you not be accepted? But if you do not do what is right, sin is crouching at your door; it desires to have you, but you must master it." Genesis 4:5–7 (emphasis added)

David committed adultery, and tried to cover up his sin. He wrote a psalm that shows the connection between his actions, thoughts, and feelings:

> My bones have no soundness because of
>   my sin.
> My guilt has overwhelmed me
>   like a burden too heavy to bear.
> My wounds fester and are loathsome
>   because of my sinful folly.
> I am bowed down and brought very low;
>   all day long I go about mourning.
> My back is filled with searing pain;
>   there is no health in my body.
> I am feeble and utterly crushed;
>   I groan in anguish of heart.

All my longings lie open before you, O LORD;
    my sighing is not hidden from you.
My heart pounds, my strength fails me;
    even the light has gone from my eyes.
My friends and companions avoid me
      because of my wounds;
    my neighbors stay far away.
Psalm 38:3–11

Proverbs 17:22 shows us some of the ways that our feelings can affect us physically. Joy heals us; disappointment tears us down:

A cheerful heart is good medicine,
    but a crushed spirit dries up the bones.

Because our thoughts affect our emotions, which in turn affect our spirituality, our happiness, and our health, God pays a lot of attention to our thoughts. God's word puts us in touch with the thoughts of our hearts, and helps us to sift through them.

For the word of God is living and active. Sharper than any double-edged sword, it penetrates even to dividing soul and spirit, joints and marrow; it judges the thoughts and attitudes of the heart. Hebrews 4:12

No wonder Solomon, the wisest man who lived, gave us this instruction to guard our hearts, the storage place of our thoughts:

Guard your heart above all else,

for it determines the course of your life.
Proverbs 4:23 (NLT)

Changing Our Thinking

The Bible calls us to control our emotions: "Be joyful always" (1 Thessalonians 5:16); "Do not be afraid" (Luke 12:32 and multiple other places); "Do not be anxious about anything" (Philippians 4:6); and we could list many more similar passages. Therefore, there must be a way for us to influence our emotions. Where do we start in order to be successful in controlling our emotions? We learn from the Scriptures that we must take our thoughts captive and make them obedient to Christ.

> For though we live in the world, we do not wage war as the world does. The weapons we fight with are not the weapons of the world. On the contrary, they have divine power to demolish strongholds. We demolish arguments and every pretension that sets itself up against the knowledge of God, and we take captive every thought to make it obedient to Christ. 2 Corinthians 10:3–5

There are two components to this command:

1. Take every thought captive (which means *imprisoned* or *confined*).

2. Make your thoughts obedient (which means *submissive*) to Christ.

How in the world do we do this? What kind of

"thought thermostat" can we find to help us? Some of us try to close off our thoughts through all kinds of activity and entertainment. Others try to medicate negative thoughts and feelings with harmful things like alcohol and pills. Still others, in a more positive way, turn to the power of positive thinking, cognitive therapy, or other kinds of therapy. Even though these methods can be helpful, the Bible tells us that God has quite a different way he wants us to change our thought patterns. We are to use divine power to demolish Satan's strongholds.

Make no mistake that the devil desires to develop strongholds of unbelief and distorted thinking in the mind of every woman. God says we have the power to demolish every stronghold that he sets up. Do you believe this?

Identify Your Thoughts.

What does it mean, practically, to take every thought captive? First, it means that we need to become aware of our thoughts and how we think. Get to know your mental patterns. Take stock of your thought life. Our thoughts give birth to our emotions. God knew long ago that changing our thoughts can allow us to change our feelings and align them with God's ways. Consider the following passages:

> Do not conform any longer to the pattern of this world, but be transformed by the renewing of your mind. Then you will be able to test

and approve what God's will is—his good, pleasing and perfect will. Romans 12:2

So I tell you this, and insist on it in the Lord, that you must no longer live as the Gentiles do, in the futility of their thinking. They are darkened in their understanding and separated from the life of God because of the ignorance that is in them due to the hardening of their hearts. Having lost all sensitivity, they have given themselves over to sensuality so as to indulge in every kind of impurity, with a continual lust for more.

You, however, did not come to know Christ that way. Surely you heard of him and were taught in him in accordance with the truth that is in Jesus. You were taught, with regard to your former way of life, to put off your old self, which is being corrupted by its deceitful desires; to be made new in the attitude of your minds; and to put on the new self, created to be like God in true righteousness and holiness. Ephesians 4:17–24

Finally, brothers, whatever is true, whatever is noble, whatever is right, whatever is pure, whatever is lovely, whatever is admirable—if anything is excellent or praiseworthy—think about such things. Philippians 4:8

Set your minds on things above, not on earthly things. For you died, and your life is now hidden with Christ in God.
Colossians 3:2–3

> Have nothing to do with godless myths and old wives' tales; rather, train yourself to be godly. For physical training is of some value, but godliness has value for all things, holding promise for both the present life and the life to come. 1 Timothy 4:7–8

Identifying our thoughts as worldly or spiritual allows us to then take them captive.

Identify and Believe the Truth.

Just as he first did with Eve, Satan tries to convince us that God's words are not true and reliable, and that they ultimately are not good for us. In order for our thoughts to be made obedient to Christ, we must believe that God is true to his word and that he cannot lie.

Do you believe these truths about God?

- God is good (Psalm 136:1).

- God is love (1 John 4:16). If he is love, then according to 1 Corinthians 13, he is patient, he is kind, he does not rejoice with evil but rejoices with the truth, he keeps no records of wrong, and so on.

- God can be trusted. He will not leave us or forsake us. (Hebrews 13:5).

- God is unchangeable. He does not change his love for us or his promises to us based on his whims or emotions
  (Hebrews 13:8; Numbers 23:19).

- God does not lie (Hebrews 6:18).

- God is all-powerful. He has the love and the power to help us (Matthew 19:26; Luke 1:37; Jeremiah 32:27; Psalm 147:5).

- God helps us when we are tempted; he helps us find a way out (1 Corinthians 10:13).

- Jesus went before us and showed us how to defeat evil (Hebrews 4:15; 12:1–3).

If we believe the truth about God, we can then evaluate our thoughts to discern whether or not our thinking is godly, or coming from the lies of Satan. It's crucial to make this discernment and then hold on to the truths and spit out the lies.

Take Hold of Divine Power.

Second, we must believe that through the power of the Spirit (the divine power), we have the mind of Christ.

> We do, however, speak a message of wisdom among the mature, but not the wisdom of this age or of the rulers of this age, who are coming to nothing. No, we speak of God's secret wisdom, a wisdom that has been hidden and that God destined for our glory before time began. None of the rulers of this age understood it, for if they had, they would not have crucified the Lord of glory.
>
> However, as it is written:

"No eye has seen,
  no ear has heard,
no mind has conceived
    what God has prepared for those who love
      him"—

but God has revealed it to us by his Spirit.

The Spirit searches all things, even the deep things of God. For who among men knows the thoughts of a man except the man's spirit within him? In the same way no one knows the thoughts of God except the Spirit of God. We have not received the spirit of the world but the Spirit who is from God, that we may understand what God has freely given us. This is what we speak, not in words taught us by human wisdom but in words taught by the Spirit, expressing spiritual truths in spiritual words. The man without the Spirit does not accept the things that come from the Spirit of God, for they are foolishness to him, and he cannot understand them, because they are spiritually discerned. The spiritual man makes judgments about all things, but he himself is not subject to any man's judgment:

"For who has known the mind of the Lord
    that he may instruct him?"

But we have the mind of Christ. 1 Corinthians 2:6–16 (emphasis added)

If I am a baptized disciple of Jesus, I am made new, perfect—a new creation—and I have access to this divine power, which will help me identify and control wrong thinking patterns.

> So from now on we regard no one from a worldly point of view. Though we once regarded Christ in this way, we do so no longer. Therefore, if anyone is in Christ, he is a new creation; the old has gone, the new has come! All this is from God, who reconciled us to himself through Christ and gave us the ministry of reconciliation. 2 Corinthians 5:16–18

Taking Our Thoughts Captive

To take every thought captive, we must be aware of and in control of our thoughts—and not the other way around. We can't let our thoughts blow around however they please, like laundry hung out to dry, blowing in the wind. When we don't control our thoughts, we find ourselves in situations much like this one:

> A young woman goes out for a cup of coffee with her boyfriend. When she mentions to him that they have been dating for six months, he becomes very quiet. Her mind starts to flutter as she thinks, "Oh no, I've made him feel pressure and he wants to end things. But do I even know if I am really in love yet? Maybe he senses my thoughts and fears being rejected, so he doesn't know what to say—the poor tortured soul."
>
> Her eyes start to fill with tears and her thoughts keep flying. "Maybe I'm too idealis-

tic—waiting for a knight in shining armor to come riding in on a horse, while I am sitting here next to a wonderful man who I care about and who cares about me; a person who is obviously in turmoil over my girlish, self-centered idealism. I'm such a wretch. I should offer him a break from our relationship."

Meanwhile, her boyfriend (being reminded of the time frame they had been dating) remembers that he last changed the oil in his car right before their first date, and so after six months it is time to do it again. He also recalls that he needs to get the transmission checked—but he isn't sure it is still under warranty. He fears that he could not handle a large repair bill, since he is saving for an engagement ring.

Now sobbing, the girl blurts out, "I'm so sorry to torture you. I know there's no horse and no knight. Yes, let's take a break from our relationship."

Dumbfounded, the guy wonders what just happened, and why she thinks he owns a horse.

How many of you can relate this type of journey of thought? I know I can. Unfortunately, all kinds of relational difficulties and damage can result when we let our untamed thoughts flit and float from place to place.

The Scriptures teach us to be self-controlled and alert. We must make a decision to do this. It doesn't happen by accident, but with deliberate effort.

> Be self-controlled and alert. Your enemy the devil prowls around like a roaring lion looking for someone to devour. Resist him, standing firm in the faith, because you know that your brothers throughout the world are undergoing the same kind of sufferings.
>
> And the God of all grace, who called you to his eternal glory in Christ, after you have suffered a little while, will himself restore you and make you strong, firm and steadfast. 1 Peter 5:8–10

This can be difficult, because our thoughts don't operate in a vacuum. Usually, thoughts that are powerful and controlling are connected to events and experiences that have changed our lives. For example: A thought like *I'm no good* might be connected to some type of abuse that took place when you were young. This probably produced feelings of anger, mistrust, and fear. Visceral emotions like this can be powerful and overwhelming, and tough to overcome.

Satan wants us to believe that we cannot change our emotions because they are part of our DNA. This is NOT TRUE. Satan has set up a stronghold that must be demolished by the word of God. By the time we are aware of the sorry state of our thought life, Satan has spent a long time setting up his stronghold and has gone to great effort connecting the dots between our thoughts and our feelings. When we align our thinking with the truth about God, we can use the divine tools his Spirit offers us to help us take our thoughts captive. Our thinking can be transformed and set on a new plain altogether.

> His divine power has given us everything we need for life and godliness through our knowledge of him who called us by his own glory and goodness. Through these he has given us his very great and precious promises, so that through them you may participate in the divine nature and escape the corruption in the world caused by evil desires. 2 Peter 1:3–4

What are some of the divine tools we have available to transform our thinking and set our minds? What practical steps can we take?

1. Know the Bible. Study it, believe it, memorize it, and use it. What do the verses in this chapter mean? Can you really be transformed if you don't know the word of God? Remember that Satan is armed—are you armed?

In Matthew 4, Jesus quoted the Bible three times to Satan ("It is written . . .") in order to defeat him. If Jesus needed the word of God to help him overcome Satan's temptations, why do we think we can do it on our own? It wasn't simply that Jesus knew God's word, but he believed him who said it. He decided to obey God instead of following his own inclinations and temptations. He made his thoughts obedient to God by taking them captive.

> I have hidden your word in my heart
>   that I might not sin against you.
> Psalm 119:11

2. Pray. 1 Thessalonians 5:17 tells us to "pray continually." Ephesians 6:18 says, "Pray in the Spirit on all occasions with all kinds of prayers and requests. With this in mind, be alert and always keep on praying for all the saints."

3. Overcome evil with good. It is not enough to just try to get "stinking thinking" out of our minds. If you try NOT to think about something in particular, you will find that you can think of nothing else! Instead, replace that thought with something else that is good. As Romans 12:21 says, "Do not be overcome by evil, but overcome evil with good."

I once saw a sign that said, "Sometimes I sit and think, and sometimes I just sit." It can be all too easy to let our minds wander and become undisciplined mush. We need to train our minds, exercising them with godly thoughts as the Scriptures instruct.

> Finally, brothers, whatever is true, whatever is noble, whatever is right, whatever is pure, whatever is lovely, whatever is admirable—if anything is excellent or praiseworthy—think about such things. Philippians 4:8

4. Decide who you will entertain. Thoughts of all kinds will come knocking, but we don't have to invite them in, seat them at our table, and feed them a full-course meal. Instead of inviting them in and entertaining them, shut the door on them and send them away.

Knowing their thoughts, Jesus said, "Why do you entertain evil thoughts in your hearts?" Matthew 9:4

Submit yourselves, then, to God. Resist the devil, and he will flee from you. Come near to God and he will come near to you. Wash your hands, you sinners, and purify your hearts, you double-minded. James 4:7–8

5. Practice body life. Our relationships with each other are crucial when it comes to overcoming lies from Satan. That is one reason why God expects us to be a functioning part of his body, the church. We need each other. We need perspective from someone who knows us—but is also outside of our body and experience. We need help from someone who will carry the burden with us, even if it's just by offering a shoulder to cry on, a listening ear, or prayers on our behalf.

Carry each other's burdens, and in this way you will fulfill the law of Christ. Galatians 6:2

For just as each of us has one body with many members, and these members do not

> all have the same function, so in Christ we, though many, form one body, and each member belongs to all the others. Romans 12:4–5

God will constantly remind us of his love and what he has already done for us in Christ—while Satan will continue to lie to us. Who will you believe?

The next time your thoughts seem like butterflies flitting from place to place, grab a "divine butterfly net" and take them captive. If you don't, they remain vulnerable to Satan's net. God has given us the power to discipline our thoughts and feelings, set them free from Satan's hold, and enjoy the kind of peaceful mind and spirit he intended for us:

> You will keep in perfect peace
> him whose mind is steadfast,
> because he trusts in you. Isaiah 26:3

Perfect peace. Now that's a frame of mind I can live with.

Taking It Deeper:

Taking Our Thoughts Captive:

1. Exercise: Find the truth in the Bible to combat these lies.

About God:

LIE: He doesn't really love me.

TRUTH: _____

LIE: He is not really good.

TRUTH: _____

LIE: He should fix my problems for me.

TRUTH: _____

About Myself:

LIE: I'm not worth anything.

TRUTH: _____

LIE: I can't help the way I am.

TRUTH: _____

LIE: Physical beauty matters more than inner beauty.

TRUTH: _____

About Joy:

LIE: I have to be married to be happy.

TRUTH: _____

LIE: My plan for my life will make me happier than God's plan.

TRUTH: _____

LIE: Getting what I want, when I want it, will make me happy.

TRUTH: _____

There are so many more lies to combat. Expand this list, and use it to train yourself to hide God's word in your heart. Get ready to fight the devil using spiritual weapons of war.

2. Begin to keep a journal of your thought life and feelings. Evaluate them, identify their origin, and discern whether or not they are true or based on lies. Take these three steps to help you deal with your thoughts in a godly way:

   a. **Agree with God** — What lies have you believed about your circumstances and suffering?

   b. **Accept responsibility** — How has believing those lies manifested itself in the way you live (in your attitudes, actions, feelings, relationships . . .)?

   c. **Affirm the truth** — Search for the truth from God's word. Read aloud each of the truths.

Chapter 7

Taking Our Words Captive

Have you ever been on a runaway horse? It's frightening and often results in a terrible fall—that is, unless you can get the horse under control. Or have you ever seen a fire burn out of control? It can take days to put out, leaving devastation in its path. The Scriptures use both of these examples to describe the power of the tongue.

> When we put bits into the mouths of horses to make them obey us, we can turn the whole animal. Or take ships as an example. Although they are so large and are driven by strong winds, they are steered by a very small rudder wherever the pilot wants to go. Likewise the tongue is a small part of the body, but it makes great boasts. Consider what a great forest is set on fire by a small spark. The tongue also is a fire, a world of evil among the parts of the body. It corrupts the whole person, sets the whole course of his life on fire, and is itself set on fire by hell.

All kinds of animals, birds, reptiles and creatures of the sea are being tamed and have been tamed by man, but no man can tame the tongue. It is a restless evil, full of deadly poison. James 3:3–8

The Legacy of Words

Words can stay with us for our entire lives. Most of us can remember specific words spoken to us that affected us forever—some for good, some for bad.

I had acne as a teenager. I also had the last name "Whitehead." As you can imagine, my last name invited jokes about pimples, blackheads and whiteheads. I grew to hate my skin, and tried to think of ways to wear my hair completely over my face. (As you can imagine, this made it difficult to see, and walk in a straight line!) Cruel words left me insecure.

One of my very smart and talented friends has struggled with confidence his whole life, because he is still haunted by his father's words, telling him he was worthless and a piece of trash. Another friend of mine, who is quite beautiful, had a husband who continually told her she was fat and that he wished he had married someone more physically fit. His words shattered her ability to feel lovely and loved. All too often, when I am out, I hear parents and children and husbands and wives saying hurtful and hateful things to each other—

words that are certain to leave wounds and scars.

But not all words affect us for the bad. Positive words can change the course of a person's life. I gained the courage to try new things from a high school journalism teacher who wrote prolific words of praise on my papers and told me I was very creative. As I was recently going through old files in the basement, I found the paper where she had most expressed these things to me. I still have it after forty-five years. It's the only school paper I kept. Her words stuck with me and helped me to believe that I could write something meaningful for others. My husband is generous with words of praise, which helps me feel secure and believe that I can accomplish my dreams—as long as they are in line with God's dreams for me.

And of course the positive words in the Bible have changed me most of all. God's words make me feel valued and loved. His words have changed everything about me—they have transformed my view of myself and given me a purpose in life.

Deceitful words changed the course of this world when they rolled from Satan's tongue to Eve's ears, and then from Eve's tongue to Adam's ears. The Bible recognizes that words can be a problem for women, and so it gives us specific instructions about the way we speak.

> She is clothed with strength and dignity;
> she can laugh at the days to come.
> She speaks with wisdom,

and faithful instruction is on her tongue.
Proverbs 31:25–26

Likewise, teach the older women to be reverent in the way they live, not to be slanderers or addicted to much wine, but to teach what is good. Titus 2:3

In the same way, their wives are to be women worthy of respect, not malicious talkers but temperate and trustworthy in everything. 1 Timothy 3:11

The Power of Words

The old saying, "Sticks and stones may break my bones, but words will never hurt me" may have been intended to shield us from bullying or criticism, but it's just not true. Words have the power to hurt and destroy us, or to inspire us and build us up.

The tongue has the power of life and death,
and those who love it will eat its fruit.
Proverbs 18:21

Throughout time we see the power of words. The first recorded spoken words—God's words, "Let there be light"—set in motion a physical phenomenon that is beyond our understanding as they turned darkness into light. Consider the power of Jesus' words and the care he took in using them. Even though Jesus is God's Son, he carefully considered his words. How much more, then, do we need to consider our words?

"For I did not speak of my own accord, but the Father who sent me commanded me what to say and how to say it. I know that his command leads to eternal life. So whatever I say is just what the Father has told me to say." John 12:49–50

Words, the Window into Our Hearts

Our words are the window into our hearts. We must first change the things stored in our heart before the words that come out of our mouth can change. Our hearts and mouths are intimately connected.

"The good man brings good things out of the good stored up in his heart, and the evil man brings evil things out of the evil stored up in his heart. For out of the overflow of his heart his mouth speaks." Luke 6:45

If in our hearts we carry bitterness, jealousy, a competitive spirit, insecurity, self-pity, anger, fear, distrust, suspicion, ingratitude, or jealousy, then the words that come out of our mouths may take the form of gossip, slander, criticism, judgments, put-downs, unkindness, labeling, name-calling, divisiveness, cursing, obscenity, coarse joking, foolish talk, lies, and complaining.

With the tongue we praise our Lord and Father, and with it we curse men, who have been made in God's likeness. Out of the same mouth come praise and cursing. My

> brothers, this should not be. Can both fresh water and salt water flow from the same spring? James 3:9–11

Our speech should be different after we become Christians—but when we are baptized, our words don't just magically change. At baptism, we are given forgiveness of our sins and the power of God's Spirit to help us grow and change. As we grow and our hearts and minds become more like Jesus, our words also become more like Jesus' words.

> We have not received the spirit of the world but the Spirit who is from God, that we may understand what God has freely given us. This is what we speak, not in words taught us by human wisdom but in words taught by the Spirit, expressing spiritual truths in spiritual words. The man without the Spirit does not accept the things that come from the Spirit of God, for they are foolishness to him, and he cannot understand them, because they are spiritually discerned. The spiritual man makes judgments about all things, but he himself is not subject to any man's judgment.
> 1 Corinthians 2:12–15

Unwholesome Talk

Do you find yourself continually falling into patterns of unwholesome talk? If so, it is important to identify the greatest areas of temptation in your speech in order to change them. It is also crucial to understand that God is concerned with what we say and how we say it.

Some of the terms that God uses to describe godly women (as seen in scriptures we have already read) include *reverent, respectful, temperate, dignified, trustworthy,* and *faithful.* Our conversations should reflect these qualities, rather than worldly ones.

> Nor should there be obscenity, foolish talk or coarse joking, which are out of place, but rather thanksgiving. For of this you can be sure: No immoral, impure or greedy person— such a man is an idolater—has any inheritance in the kingdom of Christ and of God. Let no one deceive you with empty words, for because of such things God's wrath comes on those who are disobedient. Therefore do not be partners with them.
>
> For you were once darkness, but now you are light in the Lord. Live as children of light (for the fruit of the light consists in all goodness, righteousness and truth) and find out what pleases the Lord. Ephesians 5:4–10

> Do not let any unwholesome talk come out of your mouths, but only what is helpful for building others up according to their needs, that it may benefit those who listen. And do not grieve the Holy Spirit of God, with whom you were sealed for the day of redemption. Ephesians 4:29

Women are specifically admonished to not be malicious talkers. Satan often tempts us to justify our sin in this area. Do you ever think, "I'm just letting people know about this so that they can 'pray' for so-and-so"? Ask yourself, "Is this something my friend would want me to share, or would she rather decide for herself if she wants people to know about it? Is talking about it really the best way to help? Should I ask my friend before I discuss it with someone else?"

Or do you ever think, "I just need to talk about how I feel about the preaching (or the way the worship service is put together, or how that person hurt my feelings . . . fill in the blank), and I need to talk about it with my whole small group at church?" Often we justify talking to the wrong people because we are too insecure or too lazy to go to the right people—the people we are talking about.

Have you ever tried to compare how many negative or corrective remarks you make to your husband, child, roommates or coworkers every day, compared to how many positive comments you make? The difference may surprise you, and will tell you a lot about the kind of influence your words are having.

When we realize what a hurtful wake our words can leave behind, it should motivate us to change. God's word is certainly motivating—consider this warning from Jesus:

"But I tell you that men will have to give ac-

count on the day of judgment for every care-
less word they have spoken." Matthew 12:36

Taking Our Words Captive

Controlling our words can seem like an overwhelming task, but God does not leave us without
the power or direction to accomplish it. Just imagine the difference our lives can make when our
words are filled with what is good and right. We
come into this new life with a lot of ungodly examples and training. It takes consistently feeding our
minds with God's teachings and his heart, if we
want the words that overflow from our heart and
out of our mouth to be pure and righteous.

The Scriptures tell us to set our hearts and
minds on things above. It is important to do more
than get the negative thoughts out of our heart. We
must learn to practice the teaching in Romans 12:21
to "overcome evil with good." Have some scriptures, songs, phrases, or godly thoughts you can
readily turn to when you are tempted. Whenever I
experience heavy turbulence on a flight, I think of
Jesus' words in Matthew 6:26: "Look at the birds of
the air; they do not sow or reap or store away in
barns, and yet your heavenly Father feeds them.
Are you not much more valuable than they?" And I
sing a song I often heard my mom sing: "Anywhere
with Jesus I Can Safely Go." The lyrics are challenging yet comforting. (And don't worry, I sing it to
myself, so the air marshals don't take me away!)

I remember driving one day, and it seemed like evil thoughts and words were bombarding my mind—as if they were coming through the windshield right at me. In my mind I began to repeat the verse from Philippians 4:8 that instructs me to think of whatever is noble, pure, lovely, admirable, praiseworthy, and so on. I made myself think about wonders of God's creation and beautiful places I have been, inspiring acts of faith I have seen in my brothers and sisters, and blessings God has given me. I sang the old song "Count Your Blessings." After a while, my negative thoughts disappeared.

We can also take our words captive by filling our hearts with humility toward God and others, practicing such scriptures as Philippians 2:3–4: "Do nothing out of selfish ambition or vain conceit, but in humility consider others better than yourselves. Each of you should look not only to your own interests, but also to the interests of the others."

Our words will become encouraging and useful for building others up as our hearts become more like Jesus. Then our words will reflect the change in our hearts and will stand out as light in a dark world.

In order to have this different view of our words, we must pray to have God's perspective of love and grace. When we see people through Jesus' eyes and not through worldly eyes, we will speak to them differently. When we trust God to work in others' lives, and realize that it's up to *him* to change them, we will be more gracious in our communication. When we seek to encourage and build up, we will offer more praise and encouragement, even when we are giving constructive input.

Listen First, Speak Second.

Have you ever spoken quickly, and regretted what you said? This is a common ailment known as Foot-in-Mouth Disease. Some of us are more susceptible to it than others, but we all "catch" it at different points in our lives. In order to take our words captive, we must train ourselves to think before we speak. Numerous scriptures speak to this need:

> The heart of the righteous weighs its
>   answers,
> but the mouth of the wicked gushes evil.
>   Proverbs 15:28

> He who guards his lips guards his life,
>   but he who speaks rashly will come to ruin.
> Proverbs 13:3

> He who answers before listening—
>   that is his folly and his shame.
> Proverbs 18:13

> When words are many, sin is not absent,
>   but he who holds his tongue is wise.
> Proverbs 10:19

> Those who have knowledge use words with
> restraint... Proverbs 17:27 (TNIV)

> My dear brothers and sisters, take note of
> this: Everyone should be quick to listen, slow
> to speak and slow to become angry. James
> 1:19 (TNIV)

Two helpful phrases to practice are "talk less" and "listen more." If you tend to dominate a conversation or small group, consider what that looks like and how it makes others feel. We can always add words later, but we can't take them back when they are hastily spoken. Since anger never brings about the righteousness of God (James 1:20), waiting to talk can help you cool down when you feel provoked.

Words that Do Good

Our words have a tremendous ability to do good. Think of ways that words from others have strengthened you, and consider the ways our words can be used for good:

• We can use our words to praise God.

How often do you take time to offer praise to God with your words? This not only means a lot to him, but it also helps us remember that God is sovereign, almighty, and immeasurably big. The Psalms are wonderful examples of giving praise to God. Reading the Psalms can help us learn to praise God with our words.

It often takes practice to learn to think and speak to God and others with praise and gratitude.

- Our words can be used to claim Jesus, stand for him, and confess him as Lord.

Through Jesus, therefore, let us continually offer to God a sacrifice of praise—the fruit of lips that confess his name. Hebrews 13:15

- Our words can also be used to spread the news about Jesus.

The idea portrayed in Acts 8, where the good news spreads rapidly, is that Jesus' followers "gossiped the gospel" in a natural, grass-roots way. They couldn't help but talk about what they had seen and heard.

Pray also for me, that whenever I open my mouth, words may be given me so that I will fearlessly make known the mystery of the gospel. Ephesians 6:19

The things we say can persuade others to follow Jesus. This world and its media and postmodern philosophy are extremely aggressive in trying to persuade us to follow our sensual desires and the ways of this godless world. It is appropriate and right to use our speech to persuade others to follow Jesus. Although the world tells us that sharing our faith is not politically correct, God tells us otherwise. When we love God and love people, we can't help but speak.

With many other words he warned them; and he pleaded with them, "Save yourselves from this corrupt generation." Acts 2:40

He began to speak boldly in the synagogue.
When Priscilla and Aquila heard him, they invited him to their home and explained to him
the way of God more adequately. Acts 18:26

• Our words can give people courage.

Think of ways that words from others have put
courage into you. Likewise, we can take our words
captive and set them free to put courage into others
in many different ways.

> Learn to do right!
> Seek justice,
>   encourage the oppressed.
> Defend the cause of the fatherless,
>   plead the case of the widow. Isaiah 1:17

And we urge you, brothers, warn those who
are idle, encourage the timid, help the weak,
be patient with everyone. 1 Thessalonians
5:14

But encourage one another daily, as long as
it is called Today, so that none of you may be
hardened by sin's deceitfulness. We have
come to share in Christ if we hold firmly till the
end the confidence we had at first. Hebrews
3:13–14

• Our words can encourage others to praise
God.

Then Miriam the prophetess, Aaron's sister,
took a tambourine in her hand, and all the

women followed her, with tambourines and
dancing. Miriam sang to them:
"Sing to the LORD,
   for he is highly exalted.
The horse and its rider
   he has hurled into the sea."
Exodus 15:20–21

Then David said to the whole assembly,
"Praise the LORD your God." So they all
praised the LORD, the God of their fathers;
they bowed low and fell prostrate before the
LORD and the king. 1 Chronicles 29:20

Speak to one another with psalms, hymns
and spiritual songs. Sing and make music in
your heart to the Lord. Ephesians 5:19

I can think of numerous times when singing
hymns and spiritual songs with others has filled me
with unspeakable joy while drawing me closer to
my God.

• Our words can encourage.

What would our speech include if we were to
learn to use it to encourage others? This may be
something new for you to put into practice, but encouraging people is right and good. Sometimes, we
can assume that the people closest to us know how
we feel about them, and so we forget to use words
that encourage them. When raising our children
years ago, I learned from some older parents the
importance of encouragement. One of the most

helpful practical tools we practiced was the "ten-to-one encouragement-to-correction ratio." We tried give ten encouragements for each correction we gave . . . it forced us to be deliberate and thoughtful in how we spoke to our children (and to each other). Try incorporating this practice with your family, friends, coworkers, and classmates.

Encouragement is different from flattery. Encouragement speaks to real character issues that are meant for the purpose of building up and putting *courage into* others. Encouragement also uses words that bring comfort to the sick and hurting. It uses words of rejoicing with those who are rejoicing. And we can sometimes communicate love and encouragement with unspoken words.

Hebrews 10:24–25 tells us that it takes thought and consideration to encourage others and to spur each other on to love and good deeds. In this passage, the writer is specifically referring to the times when we meet together as the church, the body of Christ. We spend lots of time considering what to make for dinner, what clothes to wear, and how to decorate our house; let's spend more time considering how to encourage others. The eternal impact is worth it.

> Therefore encourage one another and build each other up, just as in fact you are doing. 1 Thessalonians 5:11

Never underestimate the power of your words. They can build up and tear down. What a different world we would live in if Eve had weighed her words against the truth, and been slow to speak. Only through the power of God's Spirit and the help of other people can we become women who are clothed with strength and dignity, having wisdom and faithful instruction on our tongues.

Remember that God is able to make our weaknesses our strengths (2 Corinthians 12:9–10). Envision your weaknesses becoming your strengths and commit these things to prayer. By faith, your words will bring glory to God and will be a beacon that sheds light in a dark and lonely world.

Taking it Deeper:

Taking Our Words Captive

1. Consider the power of words, and the impact they have had on your life:

   • What are some memories you have of words that have encouraged or inspired you?

   • What are some memories of words that have torn you down?

2. Ask someone who knows you to help you identify areas and relationships where your speech can be unwholesome. How can you guard your speech in those areas?

3. Make a concerted effort to listen more closely in your conversations today. At the end of the day, take some time to think back on your conversations. How did listening help you in your relationships? In choosing your words? In exercising the fruits of the Spirit (love, joy, peace, patience . . .)?

4. Think of ways you can use your words for good today to:

   • Help someone praise God.

   • Impart courage to someone.

   • Tell someone about Jesus.

   • Build someone up.

Chapter 8

Inner Beauty

Women go to serious lengths in search of beauty. According to *The Economist*, in medieval times some women swallowed arsenic and swabbed their faces with bats' blood to gain a more glowing, healthy complexion. Women have removed ribs to have smaller waists, and rubbed the warm urine of young boys on their skin in the hope of removing freckles. Beauty products, even ten years ago, were a $160 billion a year global industry.[4]

The plastic surgery industry is booming—financed in large part by women. Some of us want to defy the natural sagging and wrinkling that come with aging (and which I myself am beginning to experience as I am entering my sixties); others of us are dissatisfied with our bodies in some way. According to statistics released in February 2013 by the American Society of Plastic Surgeons, 14.6 million cosmetic plastic surgery procedures were performed in the United States in 2012, including both mini-mally-invasive procedures and surgical procedures.[5]

And yet, as Proverbs 31:29–30 so aptly states, physical beauty is short-lived: "Charm is deceptive, and beauty is fleeting; but a woman who fears the LORD is to be praised."

It is important to ask ourselves: What kind of effort do we make, how much time do we take, how much money do we spend, and how much advice do we seek when it comes to developing beauty that DOES last—inner beauty?

Inner beauty not only surpasses time, but it continually shines outward from the core of our innermost selves, resulting in a beauty that is distinctive and far superior to our world's view of beauty. Peter describes this inner beauty, and tells us that it is of great worth in God's sight. God doesn't care how much money we have to accessorize, and he doesn't evaluate us based on the structure of our cheekbones or the color of our hair. He cares about our inner self, which also reflects on the outside, and even transforms our appearance!

Have you known women who perhaps would not win a beauty contest, but are strikingly beautiful because of the godly character, confidence, and discretion that they exhibit? Kindness can make us attractive; joy can make us radiant. Peter describes this kind of beauty:

> Wives, in the same way be submissive to your husbands so that, if any of them do not believe the word, they may be won over without words by the behavior of their wives, when they see the purity and reverence of your lives. Your beauty should not come from

outward adornment, such as braided hair and the wearing of gold jewelry and fine clothes. **Instead, it should be that of your inner self, the unfading beauty of a gentle and quiet spirit**, which is of great worth in God's sight. For this is the way the holy women of the past who put their hope in God used to make themselves beautiful. They were submissive to their own husbands, like Sarah, who obeyed Abraham and called him her master. You are her daughters if you do what is right and do not give way to fear.

Husbands, in the same way be considerate as you live with your wives, and treat them with respect as the weaker partner and as heirs with you of the gracious gift of life, so that nothing will hinder your prayers. 1 Peter 3:1–7 (emphasis added)

A Gentle and Quiet Spirit

What is this inner beauty? Does this mean it is wrong to dress nicely and care about our appearance? Absolutely not. Esther received a year of beauty treatments, and the Proverbs 31 woman was clothed in fine linen and purple. Ezekiel the prophet, in the allegory of God's deep love for unfaithful Israel in chapter 16, described how God provided his beloved with beautiful, costly, embroidered linen garments; gold and silver bracelets; necklaces, earrings, and a crown; and he even remembered the shoes—beautiful leather sandals. The problem came when Israel trusted in her physical beauty instead of pleasing God.

So what is this unfading inner beauty that is of great worth in God's sight? We are told that it comes from a gentle and quiet spirit.

Gentleness, or meekness, is not a word of weakness, but of strength. The English language does not convey this well. The definition of gentleness (meekness) used in the Scriptures denotes power under control; power that is submitted or surrendered and based in humility.

Examples of this spirit can be seen in Jesus' attitude and actions as described in 1 Peter 2:23–24:

> When they hurled their insults at him, he did not retaliate; when he suffered, he made no threats. Instead, he entrusted himself to him who judges justly. He himself bore our sins in his body on the tree, so that we might die to sins and live for righteousness; by his wounds you have been healed.

Jesus could have retaliated, but he chose submission; he could have made threats, but he chose silence. Why? Because he wasn't worried about himself, or about the people hurting him; he was concerned with submitting to God's plan for his life. This harnessing of power is the same meekness that women are called to have a few verses later, in 1 Peter chapter 3: "Wives, in the same way be submissive. . . ." Jesus is our example and our inspiration.

Quiet, as defined in Scripture, refers to an inner

tranquility and stability; to inner peace and calm—being undisturbed in spirit. This can only come from putting our hope in God. The world cannot provide this and people cannot provide this. The presence of God and the promises of God are what we need to give us this inner peace. Everything else will disappoint. God never fails us.

Women with inner beauty put their hope in God to make themselves beautiful. They reflect purity and reverence, they are submissive in their spirit, they do what is right, and they do not give way to fear. Fear often keeps us from having this kind of beauty. Fear causes us to want to be in control; it makes us insecure and concerned about what others think of us.

Beautiful to God, or to the World?

This is such a different way of thinking from the world's way of thinking. Consider for a moment the advertisements and media propaganda we are bombarded with daily. "Sexy," we are told, is powerful and empowering. Younger girls want to dress older than they are, and older women want to dress like teens. Fashion and popular culture teach us that we do not need to be embarrassed if someone can look down or through our shirt and see our bra, or up our skirt and see our thong panties. Many women try to imitate this sensual way of dressing because celebrities—women who are deemed beautiful, powerful, famous, and wealthy—champion it.

Women draw confidence from their ability to cause a man to desire and lust after them. This mindset can affect the expressions and posture we choose as we pose for pictures, and the kinds of photos we post on social media.

In light of this, consider what purity, reverence, and discretion mean in God's eyes. What do your clothes say about you? Who are you trying to please? Would God think you are beautiful?

> For you were once darkness, but now you are light in the Lord. Live as children of light (for the fruit of the light consists in all goodness, righteousness and truth) and find out what pleases the Lord. Have nothing to do with the fruitless deeds of darkness, but rather expose them. For it is shameful even to mention what the disobedient do in secret. . . .
>
> Be very careful, then, how you live—not as unwise but as wise, making the most of every opportunity, because the days are evil. Therefore do not be foolish, but understand what the Lord's will is. Ephesians 5:8–12,15–17

How timely the prophet Jeremiah's words remain:

> " 'They dress the wound of my people
>   as though it were not serious.
> "Peace, peace," they say,
>   when there is no peace.
> Are they ashamed of their loathsome
>   conduct?

> No, they have no shame at all;
> they do not even know how to blush.
> So they will fall among the fallen;
> they will be brought down when they are
>   punished,
> says the Lord.' " Jeremiah 8:11–12

We can be well-dressed and physically beautiful, but if we misuse our beauty, the Bible describes us as a pig wearing beautiful jewelry: "Like a gold ring in a pig's snout is a beautiful woman who shows no discretion" (Proverbs 11:22). Now that is a picture to ponder!

Do you think about verses like these when you choose what you will wear? Most men are tempted to lust because of what they see. (Sometimes we underestimate the power our appearance can have, because most women are tempted to lust not by what we see, but by the attention we can receive.) As Christian women, striving to protect and help our brothers in Christ, we must consider carefully how we dress. Whenever we wear tight-fitting clothes or clothes made of thin, stretchy material, we tempt others to lust. Whenever we use sensual body language that draws attention to our breasts, backside, and thighs, we tempt others to lust. Are you part of the solution, or part of the problem? Do you remember how to blush?

Inner beauty affects not only the way we live, but also the way we talk, the self-control we demonstrate, and the way we interact with the people closest to us. Inner beauty shows "God in us" to people around us, and proclaims the word of God to the world.

Becoming Learners and Teachers

God has a plan to help us develop the inner beauty he treasures. It doesn't happen accidentally or automatically. We need his word, his Spirit, and other people to help us.

> Likewise, teach the older women to be reverent in the way they live, not to be slanderers or addicted to much wine, but to teach what is good. Then they can train the younger women to love their husbands and children, to be self-controlled and pure, to be busy at home, to be kind, and to be subject to their husbands, so that no one will malign the word of God. Titus 2:3–5

Developing inner beauty is so much easier when we can watch and follow people who are living this way. We need training to help us grow in the ways we think and speak and view ourselves; in learning to do good deeds; and in the ways we love our husband and children. When I was a young Christian I loved wearing very short dresses. I had a birthmark on my thigh that I used as a marker for the length of my skirts. I felt that this particular length (or lack thereof) made my knobby knees less conspicuous. But after I'd been a disciple for a little while, a more mature Christian lovingly took me aside and asked me if I knew that my way of dressing was causing brothers to stumble. They then shared the scripture in Mark 9:42 where Jesus states that it would be better to be thrown into the sea with a huge rock around my neck than to cause a believer to stumble. Yikes! I had never seen the way I dressed from this perspective. I had been more concerned with fashion than purity . . . more concerned with outward beauty than inner beauty. After that conversation, I went home and let the hem out of all my dresses and quit wearing questionable clothing. I am so grateful to the friend who helped me to make that change!

Later in life, as a new mom, some of the older sisters at church helped me to realize that my firstborn was expecting me to obey her, rather than the other way around. Their observations helped me to begin parenting in a stronger way, and helped me to lay a foundation of respect in the heart of my children. So many people I admire—some of them peers, some "older women," some "younger women"—have helped me (and still help me!) along the way, teaching me how to better follow God and love my family, and I will always be grateful for their wisdom and examples.

Training requires initiative and humility. It's difficult to ask others for help, especially when we are working through personal problems in our character, or questions and issues in our marriage and parenting. We must be humble enough to ask for help.

How eager are you to learn? Are you allowing God's Spirit to influence you more and more? Do you seek out more mature women who demonstrate the qualities of inner beauty in order to learn from them?

If you are an older woman who has been striving to cultivate inner beauty, are you actively training younger women around you, or do you consider their lives none of your business? One of my greatest joys comes from studying the Bible with teenagers and sharing many of the life lessons God has taught me. I also find great satisfaction through helping women find peace in their marriages and gain confidence as they raise their children. Sometimes this means that I "stick my nose in their lives," but most of the time, I am invited in. It's a wonderful feeling, knowing that the lessons God has taught me—even the mistakes I've made—can help others to draw near to him.

Satan began with Eve, and he is still in the business of deceiving women. He works hard to distort the image of God in us, and he lures us to believe the lies of this world. The world devalues inner beauty, viewing it as weak and insignificant, instead of as the quiet strength and power it truly is.

It will take courage, faith, and dedicated effort for each of us to become the women God created us to be. But it is worth it. As our inner beauty grows, God rejoices—and we rejoice, too. There is something wonderful about feeling yourself grow, knowing that you are doing—and being—all that you were created for. As our inner beauty grows, somewhere deep in our hearts, we can almost hear our Father's voice whispering, "You are beautiful, you are loved, and you are mine."

Taking It Deeper:

Inner Beauty

Reflect on the following questions:

1. What do you consider beautiful in a woman? Compare the time you spend on physical beauty each day compared to the time you put into cultivating your spiritual, inner beauty each day. Does this reflect God's priorities? How can you devote more focus to developing your inner beauty? What specific characteristic would be a good place to start?

2. What are some of your insecurities about yourself? What is one specific way you can overcome one insecurity? What scriptures apply to that insecurity?

3. What qualities of a quiet and gentle spirit are easiest for you to reflect, and which do not come naturally?

4. Would spiritually mature brothers have confidence that you will always dress modestly?

5. Whose influence do you seek out to help you grow in the qualities of inner beauty? In what areas of life do you most need a godly example to follow?

6. If you are a more mature sister, are you involved in training the younger women as instructed in Titus 2? Are there any young women around you that you can befriend and influence for God?

Chapter 9

Created for Relationships

I try to imagine the moment when God put Adam to sleep so he could painlessly take one of his ribs to form the first woman. Did God already know what she would look like as he prepared to form her body? I wonder how long it took him to shape her lips and weave her hair. Perhaps God spoke to her as he worked, or perhaps he even sang to her. After he breathed life into her, I wonder if their eyes met and if she knew she had just come to life. I can surmise, from reading the account of creation, that she knew she was God's creation—and bone of Adam's bone and flesh of his flesh. It would have been clear to her that she was a part of a community. She wasn't alone—because God was there and so was Adam. She was created to be a completer, a helper—and to be a vital part of this divine relationship with God and her husband. We are all created to be in relationships. Jesus stated that the greatest commandment is to love God and to love your neighbor as yourself (Matthew 22:34–41). He also gave us a "new command" to love one another as he has loved us (John 13:34).

Even though we were created to live in harmonious union, we can see early on in the Bible a struggle to keep unity in relationships. This disunity can always be traced back to Satan's involvement with us, and the lies he tells. Even when there were no other humans around to complicate things, Adam and Eve nearly lost their relationship with God, because Eve believed Satan's lie. And then Eve's first two children, Cain and Abel, could not keep unity in their relationship when Cain, succumbing to Satan's temptation, grew jealous and resentful of his brother, who was striving to please God. As a result, Cain killed his brother. To this day, Satan continues to go after us, desiring to separate us from God and from each other. We all need help from God to build and maintain our relationships. When Satan targets women's relationships, he often tempts us with things like distrust, envy, and insecurity.

Jesus Demonstrates Relationships.

Jesus provides the help we need for developing and strengthening relationships. His life teaches us how relationships can be built and sustained. He commands us to follow his example of love in our relationships. Notice that this is a command, not just a "nice idea."

> A new command I give you: Love one an-
> other. **As I have loved you**, so you must love
> one another. By this all men will know that
> you are my disciples, if you love one another.
> John 13:34–35 (emphasis added)

What a high calling to love as Jesus loved! People will know that we are his disciples by our demonstration of this type of love for our fellow Christians. God does not say people will know we are disciples by our prayer life, or by how much we read the Bible. They will see and know that we are his disciples by our relationships with each other—our love for each other.

Jesus loved us sacrificially. He gave up the perfection of heaven to come down to earth in order to be with mankind. He served people, spent his days and nights with them, ate and drank with them, prayed with them, taught them patiently, put up with their weaknesses and sins, always spoke the truth to them, let them be part of his struggles, endured rejection and denial—and in the end he died for them.

The nature of our relationships has to be radically different from the world's relationships. These spiritual relationships take decision, determination, instruction, and hard work. They take sacrifice and love. Whether we are introverted or extroverted, God calls us to love each other as he has loved us. Love is not a theory or a Hallmark card. It shows itself through our interactions with each other.

We need to be careful not to be misled by the religious world, where going to church once or twice a week without deep involvement in one another's lives is considered normal Christian practice. Even the term "going to church" is misleading since we ARE the church—we are part of Christ's body, part of the community of God's people.

Spiritual relationships must be built. Are you praying about and working toward spiritual, loving relationships? Jesus' love for others was not conditional on whether or not they loved back. In order to love like Jesus, we must decide to love regardless of other people's response to us. And we must strive to continually conform our relationships to Jesus' standards—standards that are godly, selfless, and healthy. We can't build something we are not aiming for. If we aim for the type of relationships God describes, we will do well.

Certainly Jesus enjoyed being with his friends while walking, talking, fishing, and just living his daily life, but he knew that his relationships could not be defined simply by what he and his friends enjoyed doing together. He was here for a purpose, as are we. He knows that we as humans are often distracted from our God-given purpose, and we need each other to help us get on track and stay on track. Jesus shows us that relationships that share the same purpose are the ones that help us fulfill God's "greatest commandment" of loving him and loving each other.

Women are especially prone to be distracted by the dailiness of life. Managing our household—especially when we have young children at home—takes so much time and energy that if we are not careful, we can neglect the spiritual relationships that help us as we go through different stages of life. There were times, when my children were young, when I felt that I knew Bert, Ernie, and Cookie Monster better than I "really knew" adult women who were spiritual. I had to make time to talk, pray, and share my heart with other women—which helped me become a better mother and wife.

If we work outside of the home, our occupations can become our preoccupations, causing us to save little time and energy for anyone outside our office doors. There have been numerous times when I have been so busy with some aspect of work that I have failed to remember Jesus, the one for whom I do everything I do. I have needed, and will continue to need, spiritual friends who remind me that busyness does not equal spirituality.

Think about your relationships as we look at several ingredients of godly relationships.

Spiritual Relationships Share the Same Purpose.

Jesus has called us all to make disciples of all nations. When we share this purpose, the petty things that can hinder our relationships become less important, as we have a greater purpose to fulfill. This is not just a purpose for the "radical" Christians. This is his calling for every disciple.

> Then Jesus came to them and said, "All authority in heaven and on earth has been given to me. Therefore go and make disciples of all nations, baptizing them in the name of the Father and of the Son and of the Holy Spirit, and teaching them to obey everything I have commanded you. And surely I am with you always, to the very end of the age." Matthew 28:18–20

> We proclaim him, admonishing and teaching everyone with all wisdom, so that we may present everyone perfect in Christ. To this end I labor, struggling with all his energy, which so powerfully works in me. Colossians 1:28

Spiritual friends help each other become more like Jesus, and help proclaim him to others. Even as you enjoy hanging out with your friends, does this ultimate purpose compose the foundation of your relationship? Are both of you most concerned with helping each other, and as many other people as possible, to make it to heaven?

The book of Philemon, as well as Romans 16, uses terms such as "fellow workers," "fellow soldiers," and "dear friends" to describe spiritual relationships. I love these descriptions, as they encompass different aspects of the qualities of love that Jesus demonstrated. In these chapters, many women are included—women like Priscilla, Tryphena, Tryphosa, and Rufus' mother.

Whenever I read about these people, I am reminded of my own fellow soldiers, fellow workers, and dear friends who mean so much to me and help me be a better soldier, worker and friend. A lifetime spent in God's church has afforded me more precious friendships than I could possibly name in a single paragraph, but I'll share about a few. I am so blessed to have my adult daughters, Melissa and Kristen, as my dearest friends; they have also become fellow workers and fellow soldiers. I am grateful to call my daughter-in-law, Leigh Ann, my dear friend and fellow worker. Together we share both a rich family life and the same spiritual purpose. Within my current local ministry—my home church, my region within the church, and my family group—I rely on and enjoy close friendships and spiritual partnership with so many sisters. We talk, pray and meet together often—studying the Bible with women, helping sisters grow in their faith, confessing our sins, praying with each other, and sharing our goals, tears, laughter, defeats and victories. These women, some who are my coworkers on the church staff and some who are in my home region—friends like Maria, Lisa, Lory, Lilian, Kris, Irene, Jen, Marcia, Deidre, Melanie, and Ruby—help me keep my life and faith current and growing. My ministry work in the mission fields of Europe, the Ukraine, and

New England allows me to encourage and be encouraged by my fellow soldiers, workers, and dear friends Carol, Lena, Annie, and Laura—together we share our faith, train leaders, pray, plan, and talk about our personal lives. Friends across the miles, like Kim, are among the sisters who help me in my walk with God as we "talk each other off the ledge" when we both face various trials. Friends from teen and campus days like Pat, Robin, Geri, and Deb, are sisters with whom I can resume deep, spiritual conversations at any time. For many years, I have gained so much strength from dear friends like Gloria, Theresa, Pat, Sheila, Gail, and Kay—what joy we found working side by side as soldiers, workers and dear friends. Although we live far from each other now, the purpose we share—and still share—allows our relationships to thrive across the miles. This is a long paragraph, and a long list—and yet it could go on so much longer! But how grateful I am to God for giving me so many wonderful women in my life. Each has shaped my walk with God in her own way. Women in the world feel lucky to have one or two close friends at their side; as Christians, following Jesus' plan for relationships, God gives us a treasure chest filled with friendships!

Women have such capacity for closeness and devotion in friendship, yet many of us struggle at times with loneliness. Engaging in the spiritual battle is one of the best ways I have found to deepen my relationships. If you feel isolated and frustrated in your friendships, or if you do not feel the need for other people in your life, it may be because you are not fully engaged in the spiritual battle. When we remember that we are in a spiritual battle and that we are fellow soldiers, we feel a need for each other, and our relationships deepen. We recognize our need for each other's support, perspective, protection, and courage. As we have seen in the Scriptures, working side by side for spiritual causes is bonding. Spiritual partnership creates and sustains the closeness and safety that we crave, and that God wants us to enjoy.

Relationships Encourage Each Other.

I cried recently as I watched a touching video of a "flash mob." The scene began with a cellist going to the center of a plaza. He placed a hat on the ground beside him. One small girl put a coin in the hat, and the cellist began to play. The notes he played did not even sound like a song—the sounds from the lone instrument were incomplete and awkward. Then, one by one, other musicians came out to join the cellist, each carrying an instrument. Each added his or her notes to the song, until eventually the sound of a full orchestra could be heard. People gathered from all around to hear the beautiful music. This, to me, is representative of the harmony that our relationships should exhibit, and of the way these relationships will draw others who want to be part of this "concert." The Scriptures are full of instructions on how we should interact with one another in the body of Christ. As the Bible teaches, every part has a function to do. Each Christian is described as a "supporting ligament." Every part is different and every part is needed. You are needed. By ourselves, we don't look like or sound like God's church. We are just a lonely cellist.

> His intent was that now, **through the church**, the manifold wisdom of God should be made known to the rulers and authorities in the heavenly realms. Ephesians 3:10 (emphasis added)

Our relationships are meant to encourage us, or "put courage" into each other. Spiritual relationships pray for and with each other. Does this describe your relationships? There are so many "one another scriptures" that show us practical ways we can encourage each other. (You will find a list of some of these passages in the "Taking It Deeper" section following this chapter.) God created us to be part of a harmonious orchestra, not to be a soloist.

Spiritual Relationships Are Honest and Real.

> Instead, speaking the truth in love we will in all things grow up into him who is the Head, that is, Christ. From him the whole body, joined and held together by every supporting

> ligament, grows and builds itself up in love, as
> each part does its work. Ephesians 4:15–16

Dishonesty is one of the greatest barriers to healthy relationships that please God and bring joy to our souls. We feel things toward someone, but then stuff our feelings. Maybe we don't bring them up because we don't want to "rock the boat." However, when we don't speak truthfully, the entire boat capsizes; when we leave the proverbial "elephants in the living room," the floor caves in! Women can struggle with gossip, insecurity, jealousy, bitterness, or a fear of conflict. God instructs us in Matthew 18:15–17 to go to one another when we feel we have been sinned against or when someone has something against us. If we can't resolve the conflict, we are given further instruction to bring others in who can help us find resolution.

Often, we are afraid to bring issues up to other people because we presume the conversation will go badly. This fear may stem from past difficult experiences within our families, with coworkers, or even within our spiritual family. But when our fears cause us to hold back from the truth, we don't resolve relationships through faith. The relationships (or lack thereof) remain stuck and can't move forward.

As we learn to speak truthfully to each another, it is important to have a godly attitude, like the one we read about in Ephesians:

> Be completely humble and gentle; be patient,
> bearing with one another in love. Make every
> effort to keep the unity of the Spirit through
> the bond of peace. Ephesians 4:2–3

It is also important to remember that perfect love takes away fear. Let's resolve to be the kind of women who aren't fearful of being honest. Let us also decide to be the kind of women who invite others into our lives, making it easy for them to be honest with us.

> There is no fear in love. But perfect love
> drives out fear, because fear has to do with
> punishment. The one who fears is not made
> perfect in love. 1 John 4:18

It is crucial that we resolve conflicts. So many relationships have been ruined by unresolved issues. This happens when honesty is avoided and apologies and forgiveness are withheld. Don't let Satan win when he tempts you to be deceitful or cowardly.

Spiritual Relationships Belong to Each Other.

The Scriptures often remind us that we belong to each other.

> Just as our bodies have many parts and each
> part has a special function, so it is with Christ's
> body. We are many parts of one body, and we
> all belong to each other. Romans 12:4–5 (NLT)

We may have several different unbiblical reactions to the fact that we belong to one another.

We might freak out, thinking, "All these people belong to *me?* I can't take care of everyone!" As women, natural caretakers who tend to feel responsible for people, we can mistakenly think we are responsible for the choices that people around us make—but of course that's not true. We cannot decide anything for anyone else—they must stand before God on their own. But we *are* called to be involved in each other's lives, because we belong to each other—to help, encourage, support, serve, teach, correct, rebuke, admonish, train, and inspire each other in our spiritual walks.

Some of us feel like we just don't belong. The Bible promises that we *do* belong, regardless of what we feel. Belonging refers to a togetherness and oneness with others. We are bonded because we have shared in the new birth and have been born into the same family. Our unity is not due to any external organization but to our common union in Christ.

In other words, we do not belong to each other because we go to the same church, but because we are united to Christ . . . and therefore we are part of the same church. If you belong to Jesus because he is your brother and I belong to Jesus because he is my brother, then you and I are sisters and we belong to one another. God knows we have a deep desire to belong to a close-knit community. He designed us that way. That's why he adopted us into his family!

We have a sense of belonging with members of our family that we don't have with others—even when we spend more time in other activities. Although some of us spend more time at work with our coworkers than with our families, we don't belong to our coworkers. We belong with family.

We can be a member of a club or association, but we don't belong to the club members. But all too often, we treat the body of Christ like the AAA (the American Automobile Association). It is there for our benefit when we need it—when our battery dies, our tire goes flat, or we run out of gas. But when we don't feel we need it, we aren't involved with it.

Where do you feel you most belong? If you feel more connected with people outside of Christ than with people in the body of Christ, then your thinking is not congruent with what the scriptures teach. (For more on this, read Romans 8:15–17; 1 Corinthians 12:12–27; Galatians 4:5-7, Ephesians 1:5,11–14; Ephesians 2:19; 1 Thessalonians 2:6–12; 1 Peter 1:22–23; 2:4–5.)

Satan is constantly at work to try to alienate us from our spiritual family. With women, he often tempts us with thoughts like these:

I think differently than everyone else.
I've sinned too much.
They can't understand me.

My background is different.

I'm not as good, spiritual, or smart as others around me.

Remember that these are lies from Satan. We DO belong, because God has adopted us into the same family.

Satan may also tempt us with prideful thoughts that distance us from people in the body of Christ:

No one else thinks as quickly or spiritually as I do.

They're slowing me down.

I can't relate to anyone here.

They're just so unspiritual and frustrating.

Even though the body of Christ is imperfect, and we all struggle from time to time, remember the grace with which Jesus treated you and me.

We not only belong to each other, but we need each other.

Evaluate the Depth of Your Relationships and Determine to Deepen Them.

Think of ways you can deepen your relationships. Who really knows you? And who do you really know? Who knows the intimate you, not just facts about you and what you are doing? At times it can feel easier to substitute heartfelt communication with social media status updates. There is no substitute for heart-to-heart engagement in the lives of our sisters in Christ, and theirs in ours. The Scriptures make clear the ways we are to interact with one another—the ways we *need* to interact with one another. Make a decision to let the real you be known, and take the time to really know your friends. Determine to take your relationships deeper.

Honest relationships involve confessing our sins to each other and praying for each other (James 5:16). Is this a practice that you acknowledge only in theory, or is it something you actually practice? When was the last time you confessed your sin with a sister in Christ and prayed together? Do you keep your "home life" or other parts of your life a secret? A spiritual relationship is one where you are lovingly honest with each other, accept each other, and know that you will call each other to be more like Jesus.

Think of ways you can serve together as fellow soldiers and fellow workers. When we share our faith together, pray together, and read scriptures together, our relationships deepen. We are bonded more closely when we go together to serve and meet needs.

God's plan for relationships is nothing short of miraculous. Through Christ, he takes people from every race, culture, class, and nation, and brings us all together in one unified body. We accomplish far more together than we ever could alone—and it is not a burden; it is a joy! Through our work, we find fulfillment and find ourselves as we become the people God created us to be. And we gain a glorious reward along the way: the precious, lifetime relationships of our "fellow workers, fellow soldiers, and dear friends." I pray that God adds many such jewels to your treasure chest over the years.

Taking It Deeper:

Created for Relationships

For Further Study:

As you read these scriptures, choose one area you want to focus on in order to strengthen your relationships.

Romans 12:10,16	1 Thessalonians 5:11
Romans 15:7,14	Hebrews 3:13
Galatians 5:13	Hebrews 10:24
Ephesians 4:2,32	1 Peter 1:22
Ephesians 5:19,21	1 Peter 3:8
Colossians 3:13,16	1 Peter 4:9

Some of the better-known friendships in the Bible include the following women:

- Mary and Elizabeth (Luke 1) How do you think these women may have helped each other as they spent time together?

- Mary and Martha (Luke 10 and John 11) These two sisters were different. How did their strengths and weaknesses complement each other?

- Ruth and Naomi (Ruth 1–3) Ruth and Naomi were different ages. How did their relationship help each of them?

Chapter 10

Dressed in Good Deeds

On cold December days like today, I dress in boots, jeans, a sweater, and a scarf. When summer comes and the weather gets warm, I'll shed the boots, sweater, and scarf in favor of sandals, capris, and a short-sleeve shirt. Every morning, depending on the temperature and my plans for the day, I go to my closet and choose something to wear. I am no fashionista, but I do try to avoid the "frumpy" look as I choose my outfit. At times I will change clothes if I don't like the way something looks or fits. (I especially hate it when clothes shrink as they hang in the closet.) While choosing my clothing for the day doesn't take a lot of my attention, there are some clothes—clothes not found inside my closet— that God wants me to spend time selecting. As I read the Scriptures, I realize that God has clothes he asks us to wear. They are beautiful clothes, and they will never go out of style. This clothing works for all temperatures and all occasions. God wants me to be dressed in good deeds. He wants all women to dress in good deeds.

> I also want women to dress modestly, with decency and propriety, not with braided hair or gold or pearls or expensive clothes, but with good deeds, appropriate for women who profess to worship God. 1 Timothy 2:9–10

What Are Good Deeds?

What does this Good Deed Clothing Line look like? Additional scriptures shed light on the meaning of good deeds:

> No widow may be put on the list of widows unless she is over sixty, has been faithful to her husband, and is well known for her good deeds, such as bringing up children, showing hospitality, washing the feet of the saints, helping those in trouble and devoting herself to all kinds of good deeds. 1 Timothy 5:9–10

> In Joppa there was a disciple named Tabitha (which, when translated, is Dorcas), who was always doing good and helping the poor. About that time she became sick and died, and her body was washed and placed in an upstairs room. Lydda was near Joppa; so when the disciples heard that Peter was in Lydda, they sent two men to him and urged him, "Please come at once!" Peter went with them, and when he arrived he was taken upstairs to the room. All the widows stood around him, crying and showing him the

> robes and other clothing that Dorcas had
> made while she was still with them. Acts
> 9:36–39

Good deeds become realities through decisions we make, not by feelings we have. Good intentions are not necessarily good deeds. Deeds, by definition, denote something that is actually DONE. Good deeds have lasting effect. Tabitha's legacy lived on in the women who were recipients of her good deeds.

I find it encouraging to note that God counts bringing up children as a good deed. Sometimes, we mothers do not recognize the high value that God places on the work we do to raise our children and train them in God's ways. Bringing up children is not for the faint of heart! Loving children and training them spiritually requires daily decisions and hard work. Mothers, as you change diapers, referee spats, comfort hurts, clean vomit, and read favorite books a thousand times, don't ever forget that God sees all of this work as "good deeds."

Even if we do not have children of our own, or if our children are already grown, we are needed by the next generation. Within the family of God, we can all help to bring up children as we mentor them—teaching them in Bible classes and taking an interest in them in conversations. All of us can participate in bringing up the children of God and teaching them his ways.

Habits of Hospitality

> Be joyful in hope, patient in affliction, faithful
> in prayer. Share with God's people who are in
> need. Practice hospitality. Romans 12:12–13

I find it comforting that Christianity begins at home. Sometimes we think we always have to go and do in order to please God; we can also please him within the walls of our home—especially when we open up the doors of our home and invite others inside.

What are your habits when it comes to hospitality? Today's world of technology and instant communication can hinder us from taking the time to practice hospitality. Through hospitality we can truly connect with people as we talk with them face to face. Hospitality is not "instant"; it takes time. However, it is not meant to be a competition or a chance to showcase our skills at decorating and culinary creation. We can be tempted to let our insecurities of "not measuring up to Pinterest standards" keep us from doing what we can do. Hospitality is not intended for self-interest, but for the interest of others. True hospitality stems from a heart that loves and a heart that cares—a heart that desires to imitate Jesus.

In the Scriptures, hospitality included things such as entertaining strangers (who sometimes turned out to be angels), and often meant providing food and lodging for traveling Christians who had been displaced because of persecution. It included furnishing supplies, cooking meals, inviting others to stay in their homes, and sometimes having the church meet in their homes. God worked in and through hospitality in Bible times—and he still works through it today. While it may look a bit different today as we must be aware of a few modern safety concerns, many of the principles of service are the same.

I fear that the practice and habit of inviting others into our homes has become something of a lost art. The impact of having others into our homes for dinner or coffee or just a warm conversation can be far-reaching. It is in our homes where we listen to people and get to know each other's families. Through hospitality we show that we care. I liken the opportunity of having people in my home to bringing a treasure chest into my home. We never know the antiques and riches that may await us as we bring others into our lives. We discover many blessings as we get to know different types of people in deeper ways.

But sometimes we may feel like offering hospitality puts us on a one-way street. We can feel more like we are bringing a bag of tricks into our homes rather than a treasure chest. Some people we reach out to may have problems and needs; they may mess up our stuff, prove to be unreliable, or even betray us. Remember, Jesus never gave and served because of what he would receive from others—he did it because he loved. There is a reason the words *hospitality*, *hospital* and *hospice* all share the same Latin root: They all denote service toward those in need. God asks us to show hospitality graciously and lovingly. It is often easier to offer hospitality to people we are comfortable with and who will repay our generosity.

> Offer hospitality to one another without grumbling. Each one should use whatever gift he has received to serve others, faithfully administering God's grace in its various forms. 1 Peter 4:9–10

Don't let your fears keep you from putting on the clothing of good deeds. If you don't know how to do things like cook an economical meal for a crowd, set a table, make a good cup of coffee, clean your house, or make people feel welcomed, you are not alone. Through relationships in the family of God, we can all learn to do these things. Take it upon yourself to learn from women who are strong in these areas. This is one of the many wonderful benefits of being in the body of Christ, where you can learn from women of different ages, with all their different strengths. The resources available to us are a treasure.

We don't have to have a lot of money in order to be hospitable. The love, concern and warm welcome that we can offer to others are worth more than anything money can buy. Over the years I've burned meals and made many mistakes, but even so, practicing hospitality has become something precious and valuable to me—as well as to the people I have invited into my life and my home. I have heard many stories of people who decided to learn about the Bible and then became Christians because at first, someone was hospitable to them. I have seen the impact that hospitality has on Christians and non-Christians alike, and I am keenly aware of the impact it has had on me.

The thing is, practicing hospitality doesn't just help other people—it helps *us*. God knows that hospitality will "grow our hearts" even as we touch the people we serve. I have grown in so many areas through practicing hospitality—I've learned flexibility, selflessness, and kindness; my eyes and heart have been opened to people who are very different from me, broadening my view of the world. I've learned that I don't have to be perfect at hospitality; I just need to practice it. And best of all, I've gained lifetime friends through the practice of hospitality.

The practice of hospitality requires planning ahead as well as the willingness to be interrupted. My husband and I try to have someone into our home for a meal or dessert or coffee each week (or at least every other week), and we make it a special point to reach out to people who do not yet have a relationship with God. When our children were young, this was also a regular part of our family life. This habit of hospitality trained our children in so many important values and practices that they still carry with them now that they have families of their own.

Hospitality requires some advance planning. My husband and I sit down with our calendars to plan the "who, what, and when" required to turn our good intentions into realities. But sometimes the need for hospitality can't be neatly planned ahead. Are you available when someone needs a place to stay, or when some other need suddenly arises? Are you quick to volunteer? This serving attitude begins with a decision to be a woman clothed in good deeds. If this is a challenge for you, open your heart to ways that you might make yourself more readily available.

While our modern day brothers and sisters in Christ do not usually travel down long, dusty roads on foot like they did in the first century, there are practical ways we can "wash the feet of the saints" today. In order to do this, we must be observant to people's needs and be willing to "get the bowl and draw the water"—to show initiative to help. Sometimes this "foot-washing" may be in the form of a meal sent to a family when someone is sick, or offering help with childcare when someone is ill or overwhelmed. It could mean sending a hand-written card or making a phone call when someone has suffered a loss. It may include visits to those who can't get out and those who are in hospitals and nursing homes. These acts take thoughtfulness, time, awareness, and decisions to follow through on good intentions.

Hebrews 10:24 tells us to consider how to spur each other on to love and good deeds. This tells me that we need to remind each other to practice good deeds. It also tells me that it takes thought and consideration to turn our intentions into realities. We can't take time to "consider" if we don't put "time to think" into our schedule of daily activities.

As a word of caution, please understand that "spurring each other on" is not meant to lay burdens on each other or meant to make us feel guilty. Our schedules, opportunities, health, and circles of influence are different—so each one's good deeds will be different. We are responsible only to do what we can. Pray for the wisdom and heart to offer what you can. We never know what doors will open for God to work when we open our doors to others.

Helping Those in Trouble

Are we quick to help those who are in trouble, or do we tend to have a judgmental attitude that assumes that people who got into trouble by themselves can find their way out by themselves? I'm so grateful Jesus didn't think that way about me—if he did I would have no hope.

God also calls us to put on the good deed clothes of helping the poor. This, too, takes time and effort. It also takes money, as those who are poor are poor because they don't have enough money! We may not have a lot of money, but we can all find ways we can give and serve. We can find ways to sacrifice our favorite coffee or something else to be able to give more to the poor. We can make an extra sandwich to give to someone who is homeless. Look for ways to be involved face to face with the poor, so you can also learn from them. I am always inspired by the woman mentioned in Mark 14:6–9 who "did what she could." I'm also challenged by the widow who gave all that she had.

> As he looked up, Jesus saw the rich putting their gifts into the temple treasury. He also saw a poor widow put in two very small copper coins. "I tell you the truth," he said, "this poor widow has put in more than all the others. All these people gave their gifts out of their wealth; but she out of her poverty put in all she had to live on." Luke 21:1–4

For a number of years I worked with an organization, HOPE *worldwide*, that allowed me to visit extremely impoverished places all over the world in order to offer aid. As I have had the opportunity to walk with the poor in their own humble settings and see what true poverty really looks like, my heart has changed. The poor need us to help them—but the truth is, we need the poor to soften our hearts and help us become more like Jesus.

Why Do Good Deeds?

Jesus went about doing good everywhere he went. He healed the sick, helped the poor, took time with the downtrodden, and wept with those who were grieving. He did these things and more because he genuinely loved people. We will do good deeds when we strive to be like Jesus. We will do good deeds when we learn to love as Jesus loved. And when we do good deeds, we bring glory to God, and draw others to him.

> "You are the light of the world. A city on a hill cannot be hidden. Neither do people light a lamp and put it under a bowl. Instead they put it on its stand, and it gives light to everyone in the house. In the same way, let your light shine before men, that they may see your good deeds and praise your Father in heaven." Matthew 5:14–16

> Live such good lives among the pagans that, though they accuse you of doing wrong, they may see your good deeds and glorify God on the day he visits us. 1 Peter 2:11–12

When we do good deeds we also lay up treasures for ourselves in heaven. This allows us to experience life that is "life indeed."

> They are to do good, to be rich in good deeds, liberal and generous, thus laying up for themselves a good foundation for the future, so that they may take hold of the life which is life indeed. 1 Timothy 6:18–19 (RSV)

So each day as you reach into your closet, remember to take out your most important clothes— good deeds. God will be glorified, and you will take hold of the life that is life indeed!

Taking It Deeper:

Good Deeds

1. Take some time to think about the needs of people around you and how you might encourage them. Pray to see these needs as you go about your day.

2. If you're feeling overwhelmed by the idea of growing in good deeds, take it one step at a time. Making a few simple changes in our schedules and mindset can make a big difference:

   - Determine a time each week that you can devote to good deeds. When you have time already set aside, it is easier to serve!

   - Schedule specific times in your schedule when you will practice hospitality. Then think about who you can spend time with during those slots. Perhaps you can have a neighbor over, or reach out to another Christian or a new friend.

   - Purchase or make some blank cards, encouragement cards, or sympathy cards. Have them stamped and ready to send as you become aware of needs.

   - Encourage someone in your small group to organize meals and/or childcare as needed for people who are sick, out of town, or homebound. Perhaps you can organize this.

- If you don't know how to prepare a meal or a table for company, search out a mature sister who is gifted in this area and ask her to teach you. If you are unsure how to organize your home in a way that makes you feel confident about having people over, ask for help. Don't be embarrassed—many sisters would take great joy in sharing their gifts with you, and this is a way that they themselves can practice good deeds!

From the Author:

Nearly forty years ago, Proverbs 31:10–31 was read at our wedding. The preacher charged me to strive to become this kind of woman. However . . . as a newlywed, instead of clothing my household in scarlet, I accidentally turned my husband's clothes pink. I watched our car door fall off of our car—after I hit the side of our house while backing up with the door open. Instead of laughing at the days to come, I cried at the "day that was." Proverbs 31 seemed so many chapters away from my life.

Over the years, I have read this passage of scripture over and over again, prayed through it, and meditated on it. Sometimes I've found it encouraging; other times I've found it overwhelming. Although at times I have stumbled, or been filled with fear, or tried to take control, or been tempted with bitterness, or been too independent, I know I have made progress from the newlywed I was all those years ago. This is because of God's grace, his Spirit, my godly husband, and the wonderful examples of women around me. My husband graciously calls me a Proverbs 31 woman, but I know I still need to grow in so many areas. I'm grateful that love covers a multitude of sins.

In writing this book, I tried to focus on areas that can help us to become more like the woman in Proverbs 31. When you combine all of the qualities we've studied in this book, they look like her! I want to inspire and challenge each woman who reads this book to strive to acquire the qualities of the Proverbs 31 woman. Don't let this scripture scare you—let it inspire you! Take to heart the promise in 2 Corinthians 12:9–10 that God can turn our weaknesses into strengths.

Visualize your weaknesses becoming your strengths. Pray and act to that end. It will happen.

Some of us try to motivate ourselves to grow and change by beating ourselves up; and while God isn't afraid to call out our sin, he more often motivates us by his love.

This book celebrates God's special love for women—his final, "very good" act of creation. As you grow in knowing how much God loves you, you will become secure and confident, better able to tell the difference between the truth of God and the lies of Satan. Notice the confidence—not pride—that this noble woman of Proverbs 31 possesses. Her confidence, in turn, inspires others to have confidence in her. As a result, she knows she has something to offer—and her life becomes about serving others, rather than proving herself.

> A wife of noble character who can find?
>   She is worth far more than rubies.
> Her husband has full confidence in her

and lacks nothing of value.
She brings him good, not harm,
   all the days of her life.
She selects wool and flax
   and works with eager hands.
She is like the merchant ships,
   bringing her food from afar.
She gets up while it is still dark;
   she provides food for her family
   and portions for her servant girls.
She considers a field and buys it;
   out of her earnings she plants a vineyard.
She sets about her work vigorously;
   her arms are strong for her tasks.
She sees that her trading is profitable,
   and her lamp does not go out at night.
In her hand she holds the distaff
   and grasps the spindle with her fingers.
She opens her arms to the poor
   and extends her hands to the needy.
When it snows, she has no fear for her
      household;
   for all of them are clothed in scarlet.
She makes coverings for her bed;
   she is clothed in fine linen and purple.
Her husband is respected at the city gate,
   where he takes his seat among the elders
      of the land.
She makes linen garments and sells them,
   and supplies the merchants with sashes.
She is clothed with strength and dignity;
   she can laugh at the days to come.

She speaks with wisdom,
   and faithful instruction is on her tongue.
She watches over the affairs of her
      household
   and does not eat the bread of idleness.
Her children arise and call her blessed;
   her husband also, and he praises her:
"Many women do noble things,
   but you surpass them all."
Charm is deceptive, and beauty is fleeting;
   but a woman who fears the LORD is to be
   praised.
   Give her the reward she has earned,
   and let her works bring her praise at the
      city gate. Proverbs 31:10–31

Beginning from the *prime rib,* you were, in fact, created with love and purpose. As Psalm 139:13–16 tells us, we are "fearfully and wonderfully made." Our frame (be it short or tall, big or small) was not hidden from God when he made us in the secret place and wove us together in the depths of the earth. God's eyes saw our unformed bodies, and all the days ordained for us were written in his book before one of them came to be.

As God breathed physical life into Eve, may he also make your heart and soul come alive—so that you will live loved, live loving, and love living as your life brings glory to God.

Endnotes

1. dictionary.com
2. C. Austin Miles, 1912.
3. http://www.cbn.com/family/marriage/adamneve_2.aspx
4. *The Economist,* May 22, 2003
5. http://www.plasticsurgery.org